SALZBUI__

TRAVEL

GUIDE 2023

Uncover Everything You Need To Know To Plan A Perfect Trip. Essential Tips and Practical Information.

Philip Jones

Table of Contents

My Salzburg Travel Experience

I had the privilege of being a visitor in the enchanting city of Salzburg, and experienced the magic that this place holds. Salzburg, nestled in the heart of Austria, is a city that effortlessly blends history, culture, and natural beauty. From its stunning architecture to its rich musical heritage, Salzburg has a way of captivating your heart and leaving an indelible mark on your soul.

As I strolled through the cobblestone streets, I couldn't help but be mesmerized by the baroque beauty that surrounded me. The towering spires of Salzburg Cathedral reached towards the heavens, as if trying to touch the divine. The Hohensalzburg Fortress stood proudly atop the Festungsberg hill, guarding the city with an air of grandeur. It was like stepping into a fairytale, where every corner held a story waiting to be discovered.

One sunny afternoon, I found myself wandering through Mirabell Gardens, a picturesque oasis in the heart of Salzburg. The air was filled with the melodic music of birds, and the flowers' vivid hues danced in unison with it. As I sat on a bench overlooking the grand fountain, I couldn't help but reflect on the beauty that surrounded me. It was as if nature itself had painted a masterpiece just for my eyes to behold.

Lost in my thoughts, I noticed a young couple walking hand in hand towards the famous Mozart's Birthplace. Their smiles were infectious, and their love for each other was palpable. It reminded me of how music has the power to bring people together and create moments of pure joy. Just like Mozart's timeless compositions, their love story seemed to transcend time and touch the hearts of all who witnessed it.

Inspired by their love and the musical legacy of Salzburg, I decided to attend a classical concert at the renowned Mozarteum. As I took my seat in the elegant concert hall, the anticipation in the air was tangible. The orchestra began to play, and the music filled every corner of the room. It was as if each note had a life of its own, weaving a tapestry of emotions that resonated deep within my soul. In that moment, I understood why Salzburg is known as the birthplace of music.

As my time in Salzburg drew to a close, I couldn't help but feel a sense of longing. This city had become more than just a destination; it had become a part of me. Its rich history, breathtaking landscapes, and vibrant culture had left an indelible mark on my heart. Salzburg had taught me that beauty can be found in the simplest of moments and that music has the power to transcend boundaries and touch our souls.

CHAPTER 1

Introduction

About Salzburg

Salzburg, often referred to as the "Jewel of Austria," is a captivating city that offers a unique blend of history, culture, and natural beauty. Nestled in the heart of the Austrian Alps, this picturesque destination attracts visitors from all over the world with its stunning architecture, rich musical heritage, and breathtaking landscapes. Whether you are a history buff, a music enthusiast, or simply someone who appreciates the finer things in life, Salzburg has something to offer for everyone.

Salzburg's rich history dates back to Roman times when it was known as "Juvavum." The city flourished during the Middle Ages under the rule of powerful archbishops who left their mark on its architecture and cultural heritage. The historic center of Salzburg, known as the Altstadt, is a UNESCO World Heritage Site and is home to numerous architectural gems. One of the most iconic landmarks is the Hohensalzburg Fortress, one of the largest fully preserved medieval castles in Europe. Its commanding position atop Festungsberg Hill offers panoramic views of the city and surrounding mountains.

Salzburg's musical legacy is another major draw for visitors. It is famously known as the birthplace of Wolfgang Amadeus Mozart, one of the greatest composers in history. Mozart's presence can be felt throughout the city, from his childhood home which has been turned into a museum showcasing his life and works to various concert halls where his music is performed regularly. The annual Salzburg Festival, held during the summer months, attracts music lovers from around the globe with its world-class opera, theater performances, and classical concerts.

In addition to Mozart, Salzburg also played a significant role in inspiring another musical masterpiece – "The Sound of Music." The iconic film was shot on location in and around Salzburg, showcasing its stunning landscapes and landmarks such as Mirabell Palace and Gardens, Hellbrunn Palace, and the picturesque Lake District. Fans of the movie can take guided tours to visit these famous sites and relive the magic of the von Trapp family's story.

Salzburg's architectural beauty is evident in its well-preserved Baroque and Gothic buildings. The Mirabell Palace, with its exquisite gardens and grand marble staircase, is a prime example of Baroque architecture. The Salzburg Cathedral, with its stunning dome and ornate interior, is another must-visit attraction. Strolling through the narrow streets of the Altstadt, visitors will encounter charming squares, colorful facades, and hidden courtyards that transport them back in time.

Beyond its historical and cultural attractions, Salzburg offers a wealth of outdoor activities for nature enthusiasts. The city is surrounded by breathtaking alpine landscapes, making it an ideal destination for hiking, mountain biking, and skiing. The nearby Untersberg Mountain provides panoramic views of Salzburg and the surrounding region. The Salzach River, which runs through the city, offers opportunities for boat tours and leisurely walks along its banks.

Salzburg also boasts a vibrant culinary scene that showcases both traditional Austrian cuisine and international flavors. Visitors can indulge in local specialties such as schnitzel, strudel, and Mozartkugel (a chocolate-covered marzipan treat), as well as explore a variety of international restaurants and trendy cafes.

The city's warm and welcoming atmosphere adds to its appeal. The locals, known as "Salzburgers," are known for their friendliness and hospitality, making visitors feel right at home. The city's compact size makes it easy to navigate on foot or by public transportation, allowing visitors to explore its many attractions at their own pace.

In conclusion, Salzburg is a truly enchanting destination that offers a perfect blend of history, culture, natural beauty, and warm hospitality. From its rich history and musical heritage to its stunning architecture and outdoor activities, there is something for everyone to enjoy. Whether you are a history buff, a music lover, or simply seeking a picturesque getaway, Salzburg is sure to captivate and leave a lasting impression.

CHAPTER 2

Practical Information

As you plan to visit Salzburg, it is essential to understand the visa requirements and entry regulations to ensure a smooth and hassle-free journey. Here is all the information you need regarding visas and entry to Salzburg.

Visa Requirements for Salzburg:

Schengen Visa: Salzburg is located in Austria, which is a member of the Schengen Area. Therefore, if you are a citizen of a country that is not exempt from the Schengen visa requirement, you will need to obtain a Schengen visa to enter Salzburg. You can travel unrestrictedly throughout the Schengen Area for up to 90 days within a 180-day period with a Schengen visa.

Exemptions: Citizens of certain countries are exempt from the Schengen visa requirement for short-term visits. These countries include the United States, Canada, Australia, New Zealand, Japan, South Korea, and many European Union (EU) member states. However, it is important to note that even if you are exempt from the visa requirement, you must still comply with the entry regulations outlined by Austrian authorities.

Visa Application Process: To apply for a Schengen visa for Salzburg, you will need to contact the Austrian embassy or consulate in your home country or the country where you legally reside. The application process typically involves filling out an application form, providing supporting documents such as a valid passport, travel itinerary, proof of accommodation, travel insurance, financial means of support, and proof of purpose of visit (e.g., tourism, business). It is advisable to apply well in advance of your planned trip as processing times may vary.

Visa Types: Depending on the purpose of your visit, you may need to apply for a specific type of Schengen visa. The most prevalent types are transit, business, and tourist visas. Each visa type has its own requirements and limitations, so it is important to carefully review the specific visa category that applies to your situation.

Visa Validity: The validity of a Schengen visa for Salzburg will depend on various factors, including the purpose of your visit and the decision of the issuing authority. Typically, Schengen visas are granted for a maximum duration of 90 days within a 180-day period. It is crucial to adhere to the visa validity and not overstay your permitted duration, as this may result in penalties or future travel restrictions.

Entry Regulations for Salzburg:

Passport Validity: To enter Salzburg, you must have a valid passport with at least six months of remaining validity beyond your intended departure date. It is recommended to check your passport's expiration date well in advance and renew it if necessary.

Border Control: Salzburg is part of the Schengen Area, which means that there are no systematic border controls between Austria and other Schengen member states. However, occasional spot checks may still be conducted by authorities. Therefore, it is essential to carry your passport or national identification card with you at all times during your stay in Salzburg.

Customs Regulations: When entering Salzburg, you must comply with Austrian customs regulations. Certain items such as firearms, drugs, counterfeit goods, and protected animal species are strictly prohibited. It is advisable to familiarize yourself with the customs regulations of Austria before your trip to avoid any legal issues.

In conclusion, if you are planning to visit Salzburg, it is important to understand the visa requirements and entry regulations. For most travelers, obtaining a Schengen visa is necessary unless exempted. It is recommended to contact the Austrian embassy or consulate in your home country for detailed information on the visa application process. Additionally, ensure that your passport is valid for at least six months beyond your intended departure date and familiarize yourself with customs regulations.

Weather and Climate

The weather and climate in Salzburg, Austria, are influenced by its geographical location and the surrounding mountainous terrain. Salzburg experiences a temperate continental climate with distinct seasons throughout the year. The city is situated in the Alpine region, which contributes to its unique weather patterns.

Salzburg's climate is characterized by mild summers and cold winters. The average temperature in summer ranges from 20°C (68°F) to 25°C (77°F), with occasional heatwaves pushing temperatures above 30°C (86°F). However, due to the city's elevation of approximately 430 meters (1,411 feet) above sea level, temperatures can be slightly cooler than in other parts of Austria.

Winters in Salzburg are cold, with temperatures often dropping below freezing. The average temperature in winter ranges from -1°C (30°F) to 4°C (39°F). Snowfall is common during this season, creating a picturesque winter wonderland. The surrounding mountains receive even more snowfall, making Salzburg an ideal destination for winter sports enthusiasts.

Precipitation in Salzburg is evenly distributed throughout the year, with no distinct dry or wet season. The city receives an average of

800-900 millimeters (31-35 inches) of precipitation annually. Rainfall is more frequent during the summer months, while snowfall occurs mainly from December to March.

The spring and autumn seasons in Salzburg are characterized by mild temperatures and changing weather conditions. Spring brings blooming flowers and warmer temperatures, with average highs ranging from 10°C (50°F) to 15°C (59°F). Autumn sees cooler temperatures and vibrant foliage as the leaves change color before falling. Average highs during autumn range from 10°C (50°F) to 15°C (59°F).

The Alps play a significant role in shaping Salzburg's weather. They act as a barrier against prevailing weather systems, causing the city to experience a microclimate. This microclimate can result in localized variations in temperature and precipitation. The mountains also contribute to the famous "foehn" wind phenomenon, which brings warm, dry winds to the region.

Salzburg is known for its frequent cloud cover, particularly during the winter months. The city experiences an average of 1,800 hours of sunshine per year, with the sunniest months being May and June. However, it is not uncommon for clouds to linger over the city for several days at a time, especially during winter.

In terms of climate change, Salzburg, like many other regions globally, has been experiencing its effects. Rising temperatures and changing precipitation patterns have been observed in recent years. These changes can impact various aspects of life in Salzburg, including agriculture, tourism, and the environment.

Best Time to Visit

The best time to visit Salzburg, Austria, depends on personal preferences and the type of experience one is seeking. However, certain seasons may be more suitable for specific interests or weather conditions.

Spring (March to May) is a beautiful time to visit Salzburg as the city starts to come alive after the winter months. The weather begins to warm up, with temperatures ranging from 10°C (50°F) to 20°C (68°F). The city's parks and gardens start blooming with colorful flowers, creating a picturesque atmosphere. Spring is also an excellent time for outdoor activities such as hiking and exploring the surrounding countryside. Additionally, this season offers fewer crowds compared to the peak summer months.

Summer (June to August) is the peak tourist season in Salzburg due to the pleasant weather and various events taking place during this time. Average temperatures range from 20°C (68°F) to 25°C (77°F), making it ideal for exploring the city's attractions on foot. The famous Salzburg Festival, held from late July to late August, attracts music enthusiasts from around the world. However, it's important to note that summer can be crowded, especially in popular tourist areas such as the Old Town and Mirabell Gardens.

Autumn (September to November) brings cooler temperatures and fewer tourists compared to the summer months. The average temperatures range from 10°C (50°F) to 15°C (59°F), creating a pleasant climate for outdoor activities and sightseeing. Autumn in Salzburg is characterized by beautiful foliage as the leaves change color, providing stunning views of the city and surrounding landscapes. This season also offers various cultural events and festivals, including the Salzburg Culture Days and the Rupertikirtag fair.

Winter (December to February) transforms Salzburg into a winter wonderland, attracting visitors with its festive atmosphere and Christmas markets. The city experiences cold temperatures, with averages ranging from -1°C (30°F) to 4°C (39°F). Snowfall is common, creating a picturesque setting for exploring the city's historic sites, such as Hohensalzburg Fortress and Mozart's Birthplace. Winter sports enthusiasts can also enjoy skiing and snowboarding in the nearby Alps. However, it's important to note that winter can be quite cold, so appropriate clothing is essential.

Currency and Exchange Rates

When traveling to Salzburg, it is essential to have a good understanding of the local currency and exchange rates to ensure a smooth financial experience. Salzburg is located in Austria, which is a member of the European Union (EU) but not part of the Eurozone. Therefore, the official currency used in Salzburg is the Euro (€).

The Euro (€) is the official currency of Austria and is widely accepted throughout Salzburg. It is denoted by the symbol "€" and is divided into 100 cents. The Euro comes in banknotes of various denominations: €5, €10, €20, €50, €100, €200, and €500.

Currency Exchange

Travelers can exchange their foreign currency for Euros at various locations in Salzburg. The most common places to exchange currency include banks, exchange offices, and ATMs. Banks generally offer competitive exchange rates but may charge higher fees compared to other options. Exchange offices can be found at airports, train stations, and tourist areas but may have slightly lower rates and additional fees.

ATMs are widely available throughout Salzburg and offer a convenient way to withdraw Euros using your debit or credit card. However, it is important to check with your bank beforehand regarding any international transaction fees or daily withdrawal limits that may apply.

Exchange Rates

Due to a number of variables, including prevailing economic conditions, current political events, and market forces, exchange rates vary constantly. It is advisable to check the current exchange rates before your trip to get an idea of how much your home currency is worth in Euros.

Several online platforms provide up-to-date exchange rate information that can be accessed from anywhere with an internet connection. These platforms include XE.com, OANDA.com, and Bloomberg.com. Additionally, many banks and currency exchange websites offer currency converters that allow you to calculate the approximate value of your currency in Euros.

Tips for Currency Exchange

- Research: Before your trip, research the current exchange rates and compare them across different sources to ensure you get the best deal.
- Timing: Exchange rates can fluctuate daily, so consider exchanging your currency when the rates are favorable.
- Fees and Commissions: Be aware of any fees or commissions charged by banks or exchange offices. Compare the rates and fees to find the most cost-effective option.

- Notify Your Bank: Inform your bank about your travel plans to avoid any issues with using your cards abroad. Some banks may block international transactions as a security measure if they are not aware of your travel plans.
- Carry Some Cash: While card payments are widely accepted in Salzburg, it is always a good idea to carry some cash for small purchases or places that may not accept cards.
- Keep Receipts: When exchanging currency or withdrawing money from ATMs, keep the receipts for future reference or in case of any discrepancies.
- Safety: Be cautious when carrying large amounts of cash and avoid displaying it openly. Use secure ATMs located in well-lit areas or inside reputable establishments.

In conclusion, Salzburg uses the Euro as its official currency, and travelers can exchange their foreign currency at banks, exchange offices, or ATMs. It is important to stay informed about current exchange rates and consider factors such as fees and commissions when choosing where to exchange your money. By following these tips, you can ensure a hassle-free financial experience during your visit to Salzburg.

Language and Communication

As a traveler visiting Salzburg, it is helpful to have some understanding of the local language and communication practices to enhance your experience and interactions with locals.

Primary Language Spoken in Salzburg:

The primary language spoken in Salzburg is German. Austrian German, also known as Österreichisches Deutsch or Austro-Bavarian, is the official dialect of German used in Austria. While it shares many similarities with Standard German (Hochdeutsch), there are notable differences in pronunciation, vocabulary, and grammar. However, most people in Salzburg can understand and communicate in Standard German as well.

Common Phrases and Greetings:

Learning a few basic phrases and greetings can go a long way in establishing rapport with locals and showing respect for their culture. Here are some commonly used phrases in German that you may find useful during your stay in Salzburg:

- Guten Tag - Good day
- Hallo - Hello
- Danke - Thank you
- Bitte - Please/You're welcome
- Entschuldigung - Excuse me

- Sprechen Sie Englisch? - Do you speak English?
- Wie geht es Ihnen? - How are you?
- Ich verstehe nicht - I don't comprehend
- Wo ist...? - Where is...?
- Prost! - Cheers!

It's worth noting that many locals in Salzburg have a good command of English, especially those working in the tourism industry. However, making an effort to speak a few basic phrases in German will be greatly appreciated by the locals and can help you navigate through the city more smoothly.

Tips for Effective Communication:

- Learn Basic German: While English is widely spoken, especially in tourist areas, learning a few basic German phrases will make your interactions with locals more enjoyable. Consider taking a language course or using language learning apps to familiarize yourself with the basics.
- Be Polite and Respectful: Austrians value politeness and respect in their interactions. Remember to greet people with a smile and use polite phrases such as "Bitte" (please) and "Danke" (thank you). It is also customary to address people using their titles (Herr for Mr., Frau for Mrs. /Ms.) unless invited to use their first name.

- Nonverbal Communication: Pay attention to nonverbal signs including tone of voice, body language, and facial expressions. Austrians tend to be more reserved and may appreciate a more formal approach initially. Maintain eye contact while conversing, as it is seen as a sign of attentiveness.

- Use English When Necessary: If you encounter difficulties in communicating in German, most locals will be able to switch to English to assist you. However, it is polite to ask if they speak English by saying "Sprechen Sie Englisch?" before assuming they do.

- Embrace Cultural Differences: Salzburg has its own unique cultural customs and traditions. Take the time to learn about them and show respect for local customs, such as removing your shoes when entering someone's home or addressing older individuals with more formality.

- Use Technology: In this digital age, having translation apps or language dictionaries on your smartphone can be incredibly helpful when faced with language barriers. These tools can assist you in translating signs, menus, or any other written text you may come across.

Salzburg is a welcoming city that embraces visitors from all over the world. By making an effort to learn a few basic phrases and understanding the local communication customs, you will be able to connect with locals on a deeper level and have a more enriching experience during your time in Salzburg.

What to Pack

When packing for a trip to Salzburg, it is important to consider the weather, activities planned, and the duration of your stay. Salzburg, located in Austria, experiences a temperate climate with distinct seasons. Here is a comprehensive list of items to pack for your trip to Salzburg:

Clothing:

- Layered clothing: As the weather in Salzburg can be unpredictable, it is advisable to pack clothes that can be layered. This will allow you to adjust your clothing according to the temperature changes throughout the day.
- Warm sweaters or jackets: Even during the summer months, evenings in Salzburg can be cool. Packing a warm sweater or jacket is essential to stay comfortable during chilly nights.
- Rain gear: Salzburg receives a fair amount of rainfall throughout the year. It is recommended to pack a waterproof jacket or umbrella to stay dry during unexpected showers.
- Comfortable walking shoes: Salzburg is a city best explored on foot. Make sure to pack comfortable walking

shoes or sneakers to navigate the city's cobblestone streets and hilly terrain.

- Swimwear: If you are visiting during the summer months, consider packing swimwear as there are several lakes and swimming pools in and around Salzburg where you can cool off.

Accessories:

- Sun protection: Salzburg experiences sunny days, especially during the summer. Don't forget to pack sunglasses, a hat, and sunscreen to protect yourself from harmful UV rays.
- Adapters and chargers: If you are traveling from a country with different electrical outlets, make sure to pack adapters for your electronic devices. Additionally, don't forget to bring chargers for all your gadgets.
- Travel documents: It is crucial to carry your passport, visa (if required), travel insurance documents, and any other necessary identification or travel documents.
- Money and cards: Remember to bring some cash in the local currency (Euros) for small expenses. It is also advisable to carry a credit or debit card for larger purchases or emergencies.

- Reusable water bottle: Salzburg has many drinking fountains with fresh mountain water. Carrying a reusable water bottle will help you stay hydrated while reducing plastic waste.

Miscellaneous:

- Prescription drugs and first aid kit: If you need to take any prescription drugs, make sure you have enough for the duration of your trip. It is also wise to pack a basic first aid kit with essentials such as band-aids, pain relievers, and any personal medications.
- Travel guidebook or map: While Salzburg is relatively easy to navigate, having a travel guidebook or map can be helpful in exploring the city's attractions and finding your way around.
- Camera and memory cards: Salzburg is a picturesque city with stunning landscapes and architecture. Don't forget to pack your camera and extra memory cards to capture the beautiful moments during your trip.
- Reusable bag: Carrying a foldable reusable bag can come in handy for shopping or carrying any souvenirs you may purchase during your stay.

Remember to pack according to the duration of your trip and personal preferences. It is always a good idea to check the weather forecast closer to your departure date to make any necessary adjustments to your packing list.

Medical Facilities and Emergency Numbers in Salzburg

Salzburg boasts a well-developed healthcare system with numerous medical facilities catering to both residents and tourists. These facilities offer a wide range of services, including general medical care, emergency treatment, specialized treatments, and more.

Here are some notable medical facilities in Salzburg:

University Hospital of Salzburg (Landeskrankenhaus Salzburg): As one of the largest hospitals in the region, the University Hospital of Salzburg provides comprehensive medical care across various specialties. It offers emergency services, outpatient clinics, surgical procedures, diagnostic imaging, and laboratory services. The hospital is equipped with state-of-the-art technology and staffed by highly skilled medical professionals.

Paracelsus Medical University Hospital (PMU): PMU is another prominent medical facility in Salzburg that offers a wide range of healthcare services. It provides specialized treatments in areas such as cardiology, oncology, neurology, orthopedics, and more. The hospital has modern facilities and a team of experienced doctors who deliver high-quality care to patients.

Private Clinics: In addition to public hospitals, Salzburg also has several private clinics that cater to both locals and tourists. These clinics offer various medical services, including general consultations, specialized treatments, dental care, and cosmetic procedures. Some well-known private clinics in Salzburg include Privatklinik Wehrle-Diakonissen and Privatklinik Villach.

Emergency Numbers in Salzburg:

In case of emergencies or urgent medical assistance while in Salzburg, it is crucial to be familiar with the local emergency numbers.

Here are the essential emergency contact numbers in Salzburg:

- Emergency Medical Services (Rettungsdienst): To request an ambulance or emergency medical assistance, dial 144. This number connects you to the emergency medical services, who will dispatch an ambulance to your location promptly.
- Police (Polizei): For any non-medical emergencies, such as reporting a crime or seeking assistance from the police, dial 133. The police in Salzburg are well-trained and responsive to ensure public safety.

- Fire Department (Feuerwehr): In case of fire or other related emergencies, dial 122 to reach the fire department in Salzburg. They are equipped to handle various types of emergencies and provide prompt assistance.

It is important to note that these emergency numbers should only be used for genuine emergencies requiring immediate attention. For non-urgent medical issues, it is advisable to visit a local clinic or hospital during regular operating hours.

In conclusion, Salzburg offers a reliable healthcare system with a range of medical facilities catering to both residents and travelers. The University Hospital of Salzburg, Paracelsus Medical University Hospital, and private clinics are among the notable medical facilities in the city. Additionally, knowing the emergency numbers such as 144 for medical emergencies, 133 for the police, and 122 for the fire department can ensure quick assistance during unforeseen situations.

Local Customs and Etiquette

As you plan on visiting this charming city, it is important to be aware of the local customs and etiquette to ensure a respectful and enjoyable experience.

Here are key customs and etiquette:

Greetings and Politeness:

When meeting someone in Salzburg, it is customary to greet them with a handshake while maintaining eye contact. Austrians generally appreciate politeness and formalities, so addressing people with their titles (Herr for Mr. and Frau for Mrs.) is considered respectful. It is also common to use "Grüß Gott" (meaning "God bless you") as a traditional greeting, especially in more rural areas.

Punctuality:

Punctuality is highly valued in Austrian culture, including Salzburg. Whether it's attending a concert or meeting friends for dinner, it is important to arrive on time or even a few minutes early. Being late without a valid reason may be seen as disrespectful.

Dress Code:

Salzburg has a relatively conservative dress code, especially when visiting religious sites or attending formal events. It is advised to dress modestly and to stay away from provocative or revealing attire. In general, neat and tidy attire is appreciated in most public places.

Dining Etiquette:

When dining out in Salzburg, it is customary to wait until everyone at the table has been served before starting to eat. It is polite to say "Guten Appetit" (meaning "Enjoy your meal") before beginning your own meal. Additionally, keeping your hands visible on the table while eating is considered good manners.

Tipping:

Tipping in Salzburg follows the general European practice of rounding up the bill or leaving a 5-10% tip if you are satisfied with the service. However, it is important to note that service charges are often included in the bill, so it is advisable to check before tipping.

Language:

The official language of Salzburg is German, and while many locals speak English, it is always appreciated when visitors make an effort to learn a few basic phrases in German. Simple greetings like "Guten Tag" (Good day) or "Danke" (Thank you) can go a long way in showing respect for the local culture.

Noise and Public Behavior:

Salzburg is known for its peaceful atmosphere, and it is important to be mindful of noise levels, especially in residential areas or near religious sites. Loud conversations or disruptive behavior may be seen as impolite. Additionally, smoking is prohibited in most public places, including restaurants and bars.

Cultural Sensitivity:

Austrians, including those in Salzburg, value their cultural heritage and traditions. It is important to show respect for local customs and avoid making derogatory comments about Austrian culture or history. Taking an interest in the city's cultural offerings, such as attending classical music concerts or visiting museums, is highly appreciated.

Public Transportation:

When using public transportation in Salzburg, it is customary to give up your seat to elderly or disabled individuals if needed. Additionally, it is considered polite to let passengers exit before boarding buses or trains.

Festivals and Events:

Salzburg hosts numerous festivals throughout the year, such as the world-famous Salzburg Festival. If you are attending these events, it is advisable to dress appropriately and follow any specific guidelines provided by the organizers.

In conclusion, being aware of the local customs and etiquette in Salzburg will help travelers navigate the city with ease and respect for its culture. By following these guidelines, you can fully immerse yourself in the unique charm of this Austrian gem.

Safety Tips for Travelers

While it is generally safe to visit Salzburg, it is always important for travelers to be aware of their surroundings and take necessary precautions to ensure their safety. Here are essential safety tips for travelers to Salzburg.

Research and Plan Ahead:

Before embarking on your trip to Salzburg, it is crucial to conduct thorough research about the city. Learn about the traditions, rules, and laws of the area. To prevent any inadvertent offenses, be aware of local customs and etiquette. Additionally, research the areas you plan to visit and stay in, including the neighborhoods and accommodations. This will help you make informed decisions about where to go and where to avoid.

Stay Vigilant in Crowded Areas:

Like any other popular tourist destination, Salzburg can get crowded at times, especially during peak travel seasons. It is important to remain vigilant in crowded areas such as tourist attractions, public transportation stations, markets, and festivals.

Keep an eye on your belongings at all times and be cautious of pickpockets who may take advantage of crowded situations. Consider using a money belt or a secure bag to keep your valuables safe.

Use Reliable Transportation:

When traveling around Salzburg, it is advisable to use reliable transportation options such as licensed taxis or public transportation services. If you choose to rent a car, make sure you are familiar with local traffic rules and regulations. Be cautious while driving and avoid leaving any valuable items visible inside the vehicle when parked.

Be Aware of Scams:

As a tourist, it is important to be aware of common scams that may occur in Salzburg or any other tourist destination. Be cautious of individuals offering unsolicited help or trying to distract you while someone else attempts to steal your belongings. Avoid purchasing goods from unauthorized street vendors, as they may sell counterfeit or illegal products. It is always best to buy from reputable stores and establishments.

Respect the Local Laws and Customs:

Respecting the local laws and customs is essential when traveling to any foreign country, including Salzburg. Familiarize yourself with the local laws, especially regarding alcohol consumption, drug use, and public behavior. Remember that what may be acceptable in your home country might not be tolerated in Salzburg. By respecting the local culture and customs, you will have a more enjoyable and trouble-free experience.

Stay Connected and Share Your Itinerary:

It is always a good idea to stay connected with your loved ones while traveling. Inform someone back home about your travel plans, including your itinerary and contact information of the places you will be staying at. This way, they can reach out to you if needed or in case of an emergency. Additionally, consider registering with your embassy or consulate upon arrival in Salzburg.

Take Care of Your Health:

Prioritize your health and well-being during your trip to Salzburg. Make sure your travel insurance is sufficient and covers medical situations. Carry necessary medications and prescriptions with you, along with any relevant medical documents. Stay hydrated, eat well-cooked food, and practice good hygiene to avoid falling ill during your trip.

Be Mindful of Your Belongings:

While exploring Salzburg, it is important to keep a close eye on your belongings at all times. Refrain from carrying a lot of cash or sporting pricey jewelry that can draw unwelcome attention. Use hotel safes or secure lockers to store valuable items when not in use. When dining at restaurants or cafes, keep your bags and personal belongings within sight.

Emergency Contacts:

Before traveling to Salzburg, make a note of emergency contact numbers such as the local police, ambulance services, and your embassy or consulate. In case of any emergency, knowing these numbers will help you seek assistance promptly.

Trust Your Instincts:

Lastly, trust your instincts and use common sense while traveling in Salzburg. Get out of a situation if it makes you feel unsafe or uneasy. Avoid walking alone in poorly lit areas at night and be cautious when accepting invitations from strangers. By being aware of your surroundings and trusting your instincts, you can ensure a safer travel experience.

Money Saving Tips

Like any other travel destination, it's important to plan your trip wisely to make the most of your budget. Here are some money-saving tips for travelers visiting Salzburg:

Accommodation: One of the biggest expenses while traveling is accommodation. To save money in Salzburg, consider staying in budget-friendly options such as hostels or guesthouses. These types of accommodations often offer affordable rates and provide a great opportunity to meet fellow travelers. Additionally, booking your stay well in advance or during the off-peak season can help you secure better deals.

Transportation: Salzburg has an efficient public transportation system that includes buses and trams. Opting for public transport instead of taxis or rental cars can significantly reduce your transportation costs. Consider purchasing a Salzburg Card, which offers unlimited access to public transport and free admission to many attractions in the city. Walking is also a great way to explore Salzburg's compact city center and enjoy its picturesque streets.

Food and Drinks: Eating out at restaurants can quickly add up, so it's wise to be mindful of your food expenses. Look for local eateries or street food stalls that offer authentic Austrian cuisine at more affordable prices compared to touristy restaurants. Additionally, consider having a picnic in one of Salzburg's beautiful parks or buying groceries from supermarkets to prepare your own meals. Don't forget to try traditional delicacies such as pretzels and strudels from local bakeries.

Attractions and Sightseeing: Salzburg offers a wide range of attractions and sightseeing opportunities, but visiting all of them can be costly. Prioritize the attractions that interest you the most and consider purchasing combination tickets or city passes that offer discounted entry to multiple sites. Many museums and attractions also offer reduced admission fees for students, seniors, or families, so be sure to inquire about any available discounts.

Free Activities: Salzburg has plenty of free activities and sights to explore. Take a stroll through the historic Old Town (Altstadt) and admire its baroque architecture, visit Mirabell Gardens with its beautiful flower displays, or hike up to the Hohensalzburg Fortress for panoramic views of the city. Additionally, keep an eye out for free concerts or performances that often take place in churches or public squares.

Shopping: If you're looking to buy souvenirs or gifts, avoid touristy shops near major attractions as they tend to be more expensive. Instead, explore local markets such as the Grünmarkt or the Saturday flea market at Universitätsplatz for unique and affordable items. Remember to haggle at flea markets for better deals.

Tap Water: Salzburg has excellent tap water quality, so there's no need to spend money on bottled water. Carry a reusable water bottle and refill it throughout the day to stay hydrated without adding unnecessary expenses.

Currency Exchange: When exchanging currency, be cautious of high commission rates and unfavorable exchange rates at airports or tourist areas. It's often better to withdraw cash from ATMs located in banks or use credit cards that offer competitive exchange rates and minimal transaction fees.

By following these money-saving tips, you can enjoy your trip to Salzburg without breaking the bank.

CHAPTER 3

Getting to Salzburg

By Air

Getting to Salzburg by air is a convenient and popular option for travelers visiting this beautiful city in Austria. Salzburg is served by its own international airport, which offers a range of domestic and international flights. In this comprehensive guide, we will explore the various aspects of getting to Salzburg by air, including airlines, flight options, airport facilities, and transportation from the airport to the city center.

Salzburg Airport W. A. Mozart, also known as Salzburg Airport or simply Mozart Airport, is the main airport serving the city of Salzburg. It is located approximately 4 kilometers west of the city center, making it easily accessible for travelers. The airport is named after Wolfgang Amadeus Mozart, a famous composer who was born in Salzburg.

Airlines: Several major airlines operate regular flights to and from Salzburg Airport. These include both full-service carriers and low-cost airlines, providing a wide range of options for travelers. Some of the airlines that serve Salzburg Airport include Austrian

Airlines, Lufthansa, Eurowings, Ryanair, British Airways, Turkish Airlines, and Swiss International Air Lines.

Flight Options: Salzburg Airport offers a variety of domestic and international flight options. Domestic flights connect Salzburg with other cities within Austria, such as Vienna and Innsbruck. International flights connect Salzburg with major European cities like London, Frankfurt, Zurich, Istanbul, Amsterdam, Paris, Rome, Barcelona, and many more.

Transportation from the Airport to the City Center: There are several transportation options available for travelers to reach the city center from Salzburg Airport.

- Bus: The public bus service (Line 2) connects the airport with the city center and other key locations in Salzburg. The bus stop is located just outside the terminal building, and tickets can be purchased from the driver or at the ticket machines at the bus stop.
- Taxi: Outside the terminal building, taxis are readily accessible. The journey from the airport to the city center takes approximately 15 minutes, depending on traffic conditions. It is advisable to use licensed taxis and confirm the fare before starting the journey.
- Car Rental: Car rental services are available at Salzburg Airport for those who prefer to explore the city and its

surroundings at their own pace. Several international car rental companies have counters at the airport, offering a wide range of vehicles to suit different needs.

- Private Transfers: Private transfer services can also be arranged in advance for a hassle-free journey from the airport to your accommodation in Salzburg. These services provide door-to-door transportation in comfortable vehicles with professional drivers.

In conclusion, getting to Salzburg by air is a convenient option due to the presence of Salzburg Airport. With a variety of airlines and flight options, travelers can easily reach Salzburg from domestic and international destinations. The airport offers modern facilities and various transportation options to ensure a smooth transition from the airport to the city center. Whether you are visiting Salzburg for leisure or business, flying to Salzburg provides a convenient and efficient way to reach this charming Austrian city.

By Train

Getting to Salzburg by train is a convenient and popular option for travelers visiting this beautiful city in Austria. Salzburg is well-connected to various European cities through an extensive rail network, making it easily accessible for both domestic and international visitors. This comprehensive guide will provide you with all the information you need to know about getting to Salzburg by train, including routes, ticket options, and travel tips.

Routes to Salzburg:

Salzburg is located in the heart of Europe, making it easily accessible by train from various major cities. There are several direct train connections to Salzburg from neighboring countries such as Germany, Switzerland, Italy, and Hungary. Here are some of the popular routes to Salzburg:

From Munich: Munich, the capital of Bavaria in Germany, is just a short distance away from Salzburg. There are frequent direct trains that connect Munich Hauptbahnhof (main train station) to Salzburg Hauptbahnhof. The journey takes approximately 1.5 to 2 hours, depending on the type of train you choose.

From Vienna: Vienna, the capital of Austria, is another major hub with excellent train connections to Salzburg. Direct trains run frequently between Vienna Hauptbahnhof and Salzburg Hauptbahnhof, with a journey time of around 2.5 to 3 hours.

From Zurich: If you are traveling from Switzerland, Zurich offers direct train services to Salzburg. The journey takes approximately 5 to 6 hours, depending on the route and connections.

Ticket Options:

When traveling by train to Salzburg, there are various ticket options available depending on your preferences and travel plans. *Here are common ticket types:*

- Standard Tickets: These tickets are valid for a specific date and time and offer flexibility in terms of choosing your departure time.
- Advance Purchase Tickets: If you book your train tickets well in advance, you can often find discounted fares. These tickets are usually non-refundable and have limited availability.
- Eurail Pass: If you are planning to explore multiple European countries by train, a Eurail Pass can be a cost-effective option. With a Eurail Pass, you can travel on unlimited trains within a specific period.
- Regional Tickets: If you are traveling within Austria or neighboring regions, regional tickets offer discounted fares for shorter distances.

It is recommended to book your train tickets in advance, especially during peak travel seasons, to secure the best fares and ensure availability.

Travel Tips:

Here are some useful tips to make your train journey to Salzburg more enjoyable:

- Seat Reservations: While seat reservations are not mandatory on most trains to Salzburg, it is advisable to reserve seats, especially during busy periods or if you prefer specific seating arrangements.
- Luggage: Most trains have designated storage areas for luggage near the entrance or above the seats. Make sure to keep your belongings secure and easily accessible during the journey.
- Arrival at Salzburg Hauptbahnhof: Salzburg Hauptbahnhof is the main train station in the city and is well-connected to local transportation networks. Upon arrival, you can easily access buses, taxis, or walk to your accommodation depending on its proximity.
- Train Facilities: Trains in Europe generally offer comfortable seating, onboard restrooms, and sometimes food and beverage services. However, it is always a good idea to carry some snacks and water for longer journeys.
- Timetable Information: Check the train schedules in advance to plan your journey accordingly. Online platforms such as the official websites of national railway companies

or dedicated train travel websites provide up-to-date timetable information.

In conclusion, traveling to Salzburg by train is a convenient and efficient way to reach this charming Austrian city. With its excellent rail connections and various ticket options, you can easily plan your journey and enjoy the scenic landscapes along the way.

By Car

Getting to Salzburg by car is a convenient and popular option for travelers who prefer the flexibility and freedom of having their own vehicle. Salzburg, located in Austria, is a picturesque city known for its rich history, stunning architecture, and being the birthplace of renowned composer Wolfgang Amadeus Mozart. Whether you are planning a road trip or simply want to explore the city and its surrounding areas at your own pace, driving to Salzburg can be an enjoyable experience.

Driving Routes to Salzburg:

There are several driving routes that can lead you to Salzburg depending on your starting point. Here are a list of some popular routes:

From Munich, Germany: If you are coming from Munich, Germany, one of the most popular routes is via the A8 Autobahn. The distance between Munich and Salzburg is approximately 145 kilometers (90 miles), and the journey takes around 1.5 to 2 hours, depending on traffic conditions. The A8 Autobahn is a well-maintained highway that offers a smooth and efficient drive.

From Vienna, Austria: If you are starting your journey from Vienna, Austria's capital city, you can take the A1 Autobahn towards Linz and then continue on the A8 Autobahn towards Salzburg. The distance between Vienna and Salzburg is approximately 300 kilometers (186 miles), and the drive takes around 3 to 4 hours, depending on traffic conditions.

From Innsbruck, Austria: If you are coming from Innsbruck, another popular Austrian city, you can take the A12 Autobahn towards Wörgl and then continue on the A93 Autobahn towards Kufstein. From there, you can join the A8 Autobahn towards Salzburg. The distance between Innsbruck and Salzburg is approximately 180 kilometers (112 miles), and the journey takes around 2 to 3 hours, depending on traffic conditions.

Road Conditions and Traffic:

The road conditions in Austria, including the routes leading to Salzburg, are generally excellent. The highways are well-maintained, and signage is clear and easy to follow. However, it is important to note that during peak travel seasons or holidays, there may be increased traffic on the roads, especially near popular tourist destinations. It is advisable to check for any traffic updates or road closures before embarking on your journey.

Tolls and Vignettes:

When driving in Austria, it is important to be aware of the tolls and vignettes (road tax stickers) that may be required. The A8 Autobahn leading to Salzburg requires a valid vignette, which can be purchased at border crossings, gas stations, or online. The cost of the vignette varies depending on the duration of your stay in Austria. Additionally, there may be tolls for certain tunnels or mountain passes along your route. It is recommended to carry some cash or a credit card for these toll payments.

Parking in Salzburg:

Salzburg has several parking options available for visitors. The city center has both on-street parking and parking garages. On-street parking is usually metered and has time restrictions. Parking garages are a more convenient option as they offer longer-term parking and are located near major attractions. Some hotels in Salzburg also provide parking facilities for their guests. It is advisable to check with your accommodation beforehand if they offer parking services.

Public Transportation Alternatives:

While driving to Salzburg offers flexibility, it is worth considering public transportation alternatives within the city itself. Salzburg has an efficient public transportation system consisting of buses and trains that can take you to various attractions within the city and its surrounding areas. The city center is relatively compact and pedestrian-friendly, making it easy to explore on foot.

By Bus

Getting to Salzburg by bus is a convenient and affordable option for travelers. Whether you are traveling from within Austria or from neighboring countries, there are several bus options available to reach Salzburg.

Bus Services

There are numerous bus companies that operate routes to and from Salzburg. These services provide regular connections to various cities and towns in Austria as well as international destinations. Some of the major bus companies operating in the region include FlixBus, Eurolines, and Postbus.

Domestic Bus Routes

If you are traveling within Austria, there are several domestic bus routes that connect Salzburg with other cities and towns in the country. The Austrian Federal Railways (ÖBB) operates a comprehensive network of regional buses that serve both urban and rural areas. These buses provide convenient connections to Salzburg from cities such as Vienna, Linz, Graz, and Innsbruck.

International Bus Routes

Salzburg is well-connected to various international destinations through bus services. FlixBus, one of the largest bus operators in Europe, offers routes to Salzburg from major cities in neighboring countries such as Germany, Switzerland, Italy, Czech Republic, Hungary, and Slovakia. Eurolines also provides international bus connections to Salzburg from different European cities.

Bus Stations

In Salzburg, the main bus station is called Salzburg Hauptbahnhof (Salzburg Central Station). It is conveniently located near the city center and is well-connected to other modes of transportation such as trains and taxis. The bus station offers modern facilities including ticket counters, waiting areas, restrooms, and shops.

Ticketing and Reservations

Tickets for bus travel to Salzburg can be purchased online through the respective bus company's website or at ticket counters in bus stations. It is critical to purchase your tickets in advance, especially during peak travel times, to ensure your seat. Online booking platforms like Omio and Busbud also provide options to compare prices and schedules from different bus operators.

Travel Duration

The travel duration to Salzburg by bus varies depending on the distance and route. Domestic routes within Austria generally have shorter travel times, ranging from a few hours to half a day. International routes may take longer, depending on the distance and any border crossings involved. For example, a bus journey from Munich to Salzburg takes approximately 2 hours, while a trip from Vienna to Salzburg can take around 3-4 hours.

Comfort and Amenities

Most buses operating on routes to Salzburg are modern and equipped with comfortable seating, air conditioning, and onboard toilets. Some bus companies also offer additional amenities such as free Wi-Fi, power outlets, and entertainment systems. However, it is recommended to check the specific amenities provided by each bus company before making your reservation.

Luggage Allowance

Bus companies typically have luggage restrictions in place, which may vary depending on the operator and ticket type. Generally, passengers are allowed to bring one or two pieces of luggage with a maximum weight limit of around 20-30 kilograms (44-66 pounds). Additionally, smaller carry-on bags are usually permitted onboard.

Accessibility

Most buses operating on routes to Salzburg are accessible for passengers with disabilities or reduced mobility. However, it is advisable to inform the bus company in advance about any specific requirements or assistance needed during the journey.

Safety Measures

Bus companies prioritize passenger safety and adhere to strict safety regulations. Buses are regularly inspected for maintenance and undergo safety checks before each journey. It is important for passengers to follow safety instructions provided by the bus company and wear seat belts if available.

CHAPTER 4

Transportation and Accommodation Options

Public Transportation

When visiting Salzburg, as a traveler, you have several options for public transportation to explore the city and its surrounding areas.

Buses: The bus network in Salzburg is extensive and well-developed, making it a convenient mode of transportation for travelers. The city's public bus system is operated by Salzburger Verkehrsverbund (SVV), which provides regular services throughout the city and its suburbs. The buses are modern, comfortable, and equipped with facilities such as air conditioning and free Wi-Fi. They are also wheelchair accessible, ensuring inclusivity for all passengers.

The bus routes cover all major attractions and landmarks in Salzburg, including the historic Old Town (Altstadt), Mirabell Palace, Hohensalzburg Fortress, Hellbrunn Palace, and the famous Sound of Music locations. The buses run at frequent intervals during the day, with reduced services during evenings and weekends. Travelers can easily access bus schedules and route maps through SVV's official website or mobile applications.

Trains: Salzburg is well-connected to other cities in Austria and neighboring countries through its efficient train network. The main train station in Salzburg is called Salzburg Hauptbahnhof (Hbf), which serves as a major transportation hub for both regional and international train services. Travelers can reach Salzburg by train from cities like Vienna, Munich, Zurich, Budapest, and Prague.

Within the city, travelers can use local trains operated by Österreichische Bundesbahnen (ÖBB) to reach nearby towns and villages. These trains provide a comfortable and scenic way to explore the beautiful countryside surrounding Salzburg. The train station is conveniently located near the city center, making it easily accessible for travelers.

Trams: Salzburg has a tram system that offers an efficient and eco-friendly mode of transportation within the city. The trams are operated by Salzburger Lokalbahn (SLB) and provide convenient connections to various parts of Salzburg. The tram lines cover popular areas such as the city center, residential neighborhoods, and shopping districts.

Travelers can purchase tickets for trams from ticket machines located at tram stops or through mobile applications. The trams run at regular intervals throughout the day, with reduced services during evenings and weekends. They are a great option for exploring the city at a leisurely pace while enjoying the scenic views.

Taxis: Taxis are readily available in Salzburg and can be hailed on the street or booked through taxi companies. Taxis offer a convenient mode of transportation, especially for travelers with heavy luggage or those who prefer door-to-door service. It is important to note that taxis in Salzburg can be relatively expensive compared to other modes of public transportation.

When using taxis, it is advisable to ensure that they are licensed and have a visible taxi sign on the roof. Most taxis in Salzburg accept cash as well as major credit cards. Travelers should also be aware that taxi fares may vary depending on factors such as distance traveled, time of day, and any additional charges.

In conclusion, Salzburg offers a comprehensive and efficient public transportation system for travelers to explore the city and its surroundings. Buses, trains, trams, and taxis provide convenient options for getting around, ensuring easy access to all major attractions and landmarks. Whether you prefer the flexibility of buses and trams or the comfort of trains and taxis, Salzburg's public transportation network has you covered.

Taxis and Ridesharing Services

Taxis and ridesharing services in Salzburg provide convenient transportation options for travelers visiting the city. Both taxis and ridesharing services offer reliable and efficient ways to get around, allowing visitors to explore the various attractions and landmarks that Salzburg has to offer. In this comprehensive guide, here is a detailed information on pricing structures, fare estimates, and any additional charges that may apply.

Taxis in Salzburg:

Taxis are readily available throughout Salzburg, and they can be hailed on the street or found at designated taxi stands. Taxis in Salzburg are typically metered, meaning that the fare is calculated based on distance traveled and time spent in the vehicle. The initial charge, known as the "Grundgebühr," is a fixed fee that covers the first few kilometers of the journey. The fare then rises in accordance with the distance traveled after that.

The average cost per kilometer for a taxi ride in Salzburg is around €1.50 to €2.00. However, it's important to note that additional charges may apply depending on various factors such as time of day, luggage, and number of passengers. For example, there may be a surcharge for rides during late-night hours or on public holidays. Additionally, if you have oversized luggage or require a larger vehicle, there might be an extra fee.

To give you a better understanding of taxi fares in Salzburg, here are some estimated costs for popular routes within the city:

- Salzburg Airport to City Center (Mirabellplatz): The approximate cost for this journey is around €15 to €20.
- Salzburg Hauptbahnhof (Main Train Station) to Old Town (Altstadt): The fare for this route is approximately €10 to €15.
- Mirabellplatz to Hellbrunn Palace: The estimated cost for this trip is around €15 to €20.

It's worth mentioning that these are just rough estimates, and actual fares may vary depending on traffic conditions and other factors. It's always a good idea to ask the taxi driver for an approximate fare before starting your journey.

Ridesharing Services in Salzburg

In addition to traditional taxis, ridesharing services like Uber are also available in Salzburg. These services provide an alternative to taxis and offer the convenience of booking a ride through a smartphone app. Ridesharing services in Salzburg operate similarly to taxis, with fares calculated based on distance and time.

The pricing structure for ridesharing services can vary slightly from traditional taxis. Instead of a metered fare, ridesharing services often have a base fare, a per-minute charge, and a per-kilometer charge. The base fare covers the initial distance traveled, while the per-minute and per-kilometer charges account for additional time and distance.

To get an idea of the costs associated with ridesharing services in Salzburg, here are some estimated fares for popular routes:

- Salzburg Airport to City Center (Mirabellplatz): The approximate cost for this journey with Uber is around €15 to €20.
- Salzburg Hauptbahnhof (Main Train Station) to Old Town (Altstadt): The fare for this route is approximately €10 to €15.
- Mirabellplatz to Hellbrunn Palace: The estimated cost for this trip with Uber is around €15 to €20.

Fares may vary depending on factors such as demand and traffic conditions. It's advisable to check the app for an estimate before confirming your ride.

Hotels and Resorts

For accommodation options, Salzburg offers a wide range of hotels and resorts to cater to the diverse needs and preferences of visitors. Here is a list of top hotels and resorts in Salzburg, along with their locations and costs.

Hotel Sacher Salzburg:

Located in the heart of Salzburg's Old Town, Hotel Sacher Salzburg is a luxurious five-star hotel that offers a blend of traditional elegance and modern amenities. The hotel is situated on the banks of the Salzach River, providing breathtaking views of the city's iconic landmarks such as Hohensalzburg Fortress and Mozart's Birthplace. The rooms are tastefully decorated with classic furnishings and offer all the necessary comforts for a pleasant stay. The average cost per night at Hotel Sacher Salzburg ranges from $400 to $800 depending on the room type and season.

Schloss Fuschl Resort & Spa:

Nestled amidst the stunning natural beauty of Lake Fuschl, Schloss Fuschl Resort & Spa is a luxurious retreat located just outside Salzburg. This five-star resort is housed in a historic castle dating back to the 15th century and offers a unique blend of elegance, tranquility, and modern amenities. The resort features spacious rooms and suites with panoramic views of the lake or the surrounding mountains. Guests can indulge in various activities such as golfing, hiking, or simply relaxing at the spa. The average cost per night at Schloss Fuschl Resort & Spa ranges from $500 to $1000 depending on the room type and season.

Hotel Goldener Hirsch:

Situated in the heart of Salzburg's historic city center, Hotel Goldener Hirsch is a charming four-star hotel that combines traditional Austrian hospitality with modern comforts. The hotel is housed in a historic building dating back to the 15th century and offers elegantly furnished rooms and suites. Guests can enjoy the hotel's cozy restaurant, which serves authentic Austrian cuisine, or explore the nearby attractions such as Mozart's Residence and Mirabell Palace. The average cost per night at Hotel Goldener Hirsch ranges from $300 to $600 depending on the room type and season.

These are just a few examples of the top hotels and resorts in Salzburg. There are numerous other options available, ranging from budget-friendly accommodations to luxury resorts, ensuring that every traveler can find something suitable for their needs and preferences.

Bed and Breakfasts

Salzburg, Austria, known as the birthplace of Mozart and the setting for "The Sound of Music," is a popular destination for travelers seeking a mix of history, culture, and natural beauty. If you are looking for a cozy and personalized accommodation experience, bed and breakfasts (B&Bs) in Salzburg offer a charming alternative to traditional hotels. Here is a list of top bed and breakfast options in Salzburg, including their locations and costs.

Villa Trapp: Located in Aigen, a peaceful neighborhood just outside the city center, Villa Trapp is a historic B&B that was once the residence of the von Trapp family. This elegant villa offers comfortable rooms with period furnishings and modern amenities. Guests can enjoy a delicious breakfast buffet each morning while taking in the stunning views of the surrounding mountains. The cost of staying at Villa Trapp starts at around $150 per night.

Pension Elisabeth: Situated in the heart of Salzburg's Old Town, Pension Elisabeth is a charming B&B housed in a traditional Austrian building. The rooms are tastefully decorated and feature en-suite bathrooms, free Wi-Fi, and flat-screen TVs. Guests can savor a continental breakfast served in the cozy dining area or on the outdoor terrace. The cost of staying at Pension Elisabeth starts at approximately $120 per night.

Gästehaus im Priesterseminar Salzburg: Nestled in the picturesque district of Nonntal, Gästehaus im Priesterseminar Salzburg offers comfortable accommodations within walking distance of major attractions such as Hohensalzburg Fortress and Mirabell Palace. The rooms are spacious and well-appointed, providing guests with a relaxing retreat after exploring the city. A hearty breakfast is included in the room rate. The cost of staying at

Gästehaus im Priesterseminar Salzburg starts at around $100 per night.

These are just a few examples of the many bed and breakfasts available in Salzburg. Each B&B offers its own unique charm and amenities, ensuring a memorable stay for travelers.

Hostels and Guesthouses

For budget-conscious travelers, staying in hostels or guesthouses can be a great option. These accommodations offer affordable rates, a social atmosphere, and often provide the opportunity to meet fellow travelers from around the world. In Salzburg, there are several hostels and guesthouses that cater to the needs of different types of travelers. Here are some options to consider:

Yoho International Youth Hostel: Located in the heart of Salzburg's old town, Yoho International Youth Hostel is a popular choice among backpackers and budget travelers. The hostel provides both private rooms with common bathrooms and dormitory-style accommodations. The facilities include a communal kitchen, a cozy lounge area, free Wi-Fi, and laundry facilities. The hostel also organizes various activities and tours for guests to explore the city. Prices at Yoho International Youth Hostel start at around $20 per night for a bed in a dormitory room.

A&O Salzburg Hauptbahnhof: Situated near Salzburg's main train station, A&O Salzburg Hauptbahnhof is another affordable accommodation option. The hostel features modern rooms with private bathrooms and offers both dormitory-style rooms and private rooms. Amenities include a bar, a game room, a 24-hour front desk, and free Wi-Fi throughout the property. A&O Salzburg Hauptbahnhof also provides bike rental services for guests who want to explore the city on two wheels. Prices at this hostel start at approximately $25 per night for a bed in a dormitory room.

Eduard-Heinrich-Haus: For those seeking a quieter and more peaceful atmosphere, Eduard-Heinrich-Haus is an excellent choice. This guesthouse is located on the outskirts of Salzburg, surrounded by beautiful nature and offering stunning views of the city. The guesthouse provides comfortable rooms with private bathrooms and a delicious breakfast buffet. Guests can relax in the garden or explore the nearby hiking trails. Prices at Eduard-Heinrich-Haus start at around $40 per night for a single room.

Other notable hostels and guesthouses in Salzburg include:

- MEININGER Hotel Salzburg City Center: Located near the Mirabell Palace, this hostel offers modern rooms, a bar, a game room, and a guest kitchen. Prices start at approximately $30 per night for a bed in a dormitory room.

- YoHo International Youth Hostel Annex: Situated just a short walk from Yoho International Youth Hostel, this annex provides additional budget-friendly accommodation options for travelers. Prices start at around $20 per night for a bed in a dormitory room.
- Muffin Hostel: This cozy hostel is located in Salzburg's old town and offers comfortable rooms with shared bathrooms. Prices start at approximately $25 per night for a bed in a dormitory room.

When planning your stay in Salzburg, it is advisable to book your accommodation in advance, especially during peak travel seasons, to secure the best rates and availability.

Vacation Rentals

Salzburg offers a wide range of vacation rental options throughout the city and its surrounding areas. Whether you prefer to stay in the heart of the city or in a more tranquil countryside setting, there are numerous options available to suit different preferences and budgets.

City Center: The city center of Salzburg is a popular choice for travelers who want to be close to major attractions such as Mozart's birthplace, Mirabell Palace, and Hohensalzburg Fortress. Vacation rentals in this area often provide easy access to restaurants, shops, and cultural landmarks. Prices for vacation rentals in the city center can vary depending on factors such as size, amenities, and proximity to attractions.

Old Town (Altstadt): The Old Town of Salzburg is a UNESCO World Heritage Site known for its well-preserved medieval architecture. Staying in this area allows visitors to immerse themselves in the city's history and charm. Vacation rentals in the Old Town range from cozy apartments to spacious townhouses, offering a unique experience for travelers. Due to its central location and historical significance, vacation rentals in the Old Town tend to be slightly more expensive compared to other areas.

Suburbs and Surrounding Areas: For those seeking a quieter and more relaxed atmosphere, vacation rentals in the suburbs and surrounding areas of Salzburg are ideal. These locations often provide beautiful views of the surrounding mountains and countryside while still being within easy reach of the city center. Prices for vacation rentals in the suburbs can be more affordable compared to those in the city center or Old Town.

Lake District (Salzkammergut): The Salzkammergut region, located near Salzburg, is renowned for its picturesque lakes and mountains. Vacation rentals in this area offer a tranquil retreat for nature lovers and outdoor enthusiasts. From lakeside cottages to mountain chalets, there are various options available to suit different preferences. Prices for vacation rentals in the

Salzkammergut region can vary depending on factors such as proximity to the lake, size, and amenities.

Costs of Vacation Rentals in Salzburg:

The cost of vacation rentals in Salzburg can vary significantly depending on factors such as location, size, amenities, and the time of year. It is important to consider these factors when planning your trip and budgeting for accommodation expenses. Here is a general overview of the costs associated with vacation rentals in Salzburg:

City Center: Vacation rentals in the city center of Salzburg tend to be higher priced compared to other areas due to their central location and proximity to major attractions. Prices for a one-bedroom apartment in the city center can range from $100 to $200 per night, while larger apartments or townhouses can cost upwards of $300 per night.

Old Town (Altstadt): Vacation rentals in the Old Town are often considered premium options due to their historical significance and charm. Prices for a one-bedroom apartment in the Old Town can range from $150 to $250 per night, while larger accommodations can cost over $400 per night.

Suburbs and Surrounding Areas: Vacation rentals in the suburbs and surrounding areas of Salzburg generally offer more affordable options compared to the city center or Old Town. One-bedroom apartments in these locations can cost anything between $80 and $150 per night, depending on facilities and distance to the city center, among other things.

Lake District (Salzkammergut): Vacation rentals in the Salzkammergut region can vary in price depending on their proximity to the lakes and mountains. Prices for a one-bedroom cottage or chalet in this area can range from $100 to $200 per night, while larger accommodations with lake views can cost upwards of $300 per night.

It is important to note that these prices are approximate and can vary based on factors such as the time of year, availability, and specific rental properties. Additionally, it is advisable to book vacation rentals well in advance, especially during peak travel seasons, to secure the best rates and availability.

CHAPTER 5

Top Attractions in Salzburg

Hohensalzburg Fortress

The Hohensalzburg Fortress is a prominent landmark and one of the most popular tourist attractions in Salzburg, Austria. Perched atop the Festungsberg hill, it offers breathtaking panoramic views of the city and the surrounding Alpine scenery. This magnificent fortress is a must-visit destination for travelers seeking to explore Salzburg's rich history, architectural marvels, and cultural heritage.

History and Architecture:

The construction of Hohensalzburg Fortress began in 1077 under Archbishop Gebhard von Helfenstein. It received numerous additions and renovations over the years, giving it its present magnificence. The fortress is a remarkable example of medieval fortification and boasts an impressive mix of Romanesque, Gothic, and Renaissance architectural styles.

Exploring the Fortress:

Visitors can access the fortress by taking a funicular railway or by walking up the steep path known as the Festungsgasse. Once inside, travelers can immerse themselves in the rich history and cultural significance of this iconic landmark.

Fortress Museum: The Fortress Museum provides an in-depth look into the history of Hohensalzburg. It showcases various artifacts, including weapons, armor, musical instruments, and religious objects. The museum also offers insights into the daily life of past inhabitants through its extensive collection of historical documents and exhibits.

Rainer Regiment Museum: Located within the fortress complex, the Rainer Regiment Museum focuses on the military history of Salzburg. It displays uniforms, weapons, and other military paraphernalia from different eras. Visitors can learn about the role played by Salzburg's troops in various conflicts throughout history.

Marionette Museum: For those interested in puppetry and theater arts, the Marionette Museum is a must-visit attraction within Hohensalzburg Fortress. It houses an extensive collection of marionettes, showcasing the craftsmanship and artistry behind this traditional form of entertainment. The museum also offers regular puppet shows, providing a unique and enchanting experience for visitors of all ages.

Panoramic Views:

One of the highlights of visiting Hohensalzburg Fortress is the breathtaking panoramic views it offers. From the fortress walls and towers, travelers can enjoy sweeping vistas of Salzburg's Old Town, the Salzach River, and the picturesque Austrian Alps. The view is particularly stunning during sunrise or sunset, creating a magical atmosphere that captivates visitors.

Events and Concerts:

Throughout the year, Hohensalzburg Fortress hosts various events and concerts that showcase Salzburg's rich cultural heritage. The fortress serves as a venue for classical music performances, theater productions, and special exhibitions. Attending one of these events provides a unique opportunity to experience the fusion of history, art, and music in a truly remarkable setting.

Practical Information:

- Opening Hours: The fortress is open daily from 9:00 AM to 5:00 PM (closing times may vary depending on the season).
- Admission Fees: There is an entrance fee to access the fortress and its museums. Discounts are available for children, students, seniors, and groups.
- Guided Tours: Guided tours are available in multiple languages and provide valuable insights into the fortress's history and architecture.
- Accessibility: While parts of the fortress are accessible to wheelchair users, some areas may have limited accessibility due to its medieval design.

Mirabell Palace and Gardens

Mirabell Palace and Gardens is a popular tourist destination located in Salzburg, Austria. It is renowned for its stunning architecture, beautiful gardens, and historical significance.

History of Mirabell Palace and Gardens:

Mirabell Palace was built in 1606 by Prince-Archbishop Wolf Dietrich von Raitenau for his mistress, Salome Alt. Originally known as Altenau Palace, it was later renamed Mirabell Palace by Prince-Archbishop Markus Sittikus von Hohenems in 1612. The palace underwent several renovations over the years, with the most significant changes occurring during the Baroque period under the rule of Prince-Archbishop Franz Anton Harrach.

The gardens surrounding Mirabell Palace were designed in the early 18th century by Johann Bernhard Fischer von Erlach. The layout of the gardens follows the principles of geometrically arranged flowerbeds, grand alleys, and sculptures. The garden's design was influenced by French and Italian styles prevalent during that era.

Notable Features of Mirabell Palace and Gardens:

The Marble Hall: One of the most impressive features of Mirabell Palace is the Marble Hall. This grand hall is known for its exquisite marble columns, ornate stucco decorations, and magnificent ceiling frescoes. The Marble Hall has been a venue for various concerts and events throughout history.

The Pegasus Fountain: Located in the center of the gardens, the Pegasus Fountain is a prominent landmark. It features a statue of Pegasus, the mythical winged horse, atop a fountain surrounded by four tritons. The fountain serves as a focal point within the garden's symmetrical design.

The Rose Garden: Another highlight of Mirabell Gardens is the Rose Garden. It is home to over 4000 rose bushes, including a wide variety of species and colors. The Rose Garden is particularly stunning during the blooming season, which typically occurs from late spring to early autumn.

The Dwarf Garden: The Dwarf Garden is a unique feature of Mirabell Gardens. It consists of a collection of dwarf statues, each representing a different profession or historical figure. The garden was originally created as a form of entertainment for the prince-archbishop's children.

The Hedge Theater: Nestled within the gardens, the Hedge Theater is an open-air theater that hosts various performances during the summer months. It provides a charming setting for concerts, plays, and other cultural events.

Practical Tips for Visiting Mirabell Palace and Gardens:

Opening Hours and Admission: Mirabell Palace and Gardens are open to the public throughout the year. The opening hours vary depending on the season, so it is advisable to check the official website or local tourist information for up-to-date information. Admission to the gardens is free, but there may be a fee for visiting certain areas of the palace.

Guided Tours: To fully appreciate the history and significance of Mirabell Palace and Gardens, consider joining a guided tour. These tours provide in-depth information about the palace's architecture, art collections, and historical anecdotes.

Photography: Photography is allowed in most areas of Mirabell Palace and Gardens, except for specific exhibitions or restricted sections. Capture the beauty of the gardens and palace but be mindful of other visitors and avoid using flash photography in sensitive areas.

Seasonal Events: Throughout the year, Mirabell Palace and Gardens host various events such as concerts, festivals, and exhibitions. Check the event calendar to see if any special events coincide with your visit.

Accessibility: The palace and gardens are wheelchair accessible, with ramps and elevators available for visitors with mobility challenges. However, some areas of the palace may have limited accessibility due to their historical nature.

Nearby Attractions: Mirabell Palace and Gardens are conveniently located near other popular attractions in Salzburg. Consider exploring the nearby Salzburg Cathedral, Hohensalzburg Fortress, or taking a stroll along the Salzach River.

Mozart's Birthplace

Mozart's birthplace in Salzburg is a must-visit destination for travelers who are interested in classical music and the life of one of the greatest composers in history, Wolfgang Amadeus Mozart. Located in the heart of Salzburg's historic center, this iconic house offers a unique glimpse into the early life and upbringing of Mozart.

The Birthplace of Mozart, also known as Mozart's Geburtshaus, is a meticulously preserved building that showcases the living conditions and environment in which Mozart was born on January 27, 1756. The house itself is a testament to the rich cultural heritage of Salzburg and serves as a tribute to Mozart's extraordinary talent and legacy.

Upon entering the birthplace, visitors are transported back in time to the 18th century. The house consists of three floors, each filled with exhibits that provide insight into Mozart's family life, his musical development, and his early compositions. The rooms are furnished with period furniture and personal belongings of the Mozart family, creating an authentic atmosphere that immerses visitors in the composer's world.

One of the highlights of the birthplace is Mozart's childhood violin, which is displayed alongside other musical instruments that were popular during his time. Visitors can also explore a collection of original manuscripts, letters, and portraits that offer a deeper understanding of Mozart's creative process and his relationships with family members and patrons.

The birthplace also features an audio guide that provides detailed commentary on each room, allowing visitors to learn about Mozart's life at their own pace. The audio guide is available in multiple languages, ensuring that visitors from all over the world can fully appreciate the significance of this historic site.

In addition to the permanent exhibits, the birthplace often hosts temporary exhibitions that delve into specific aspects of Mozart's life or explore his influence on music and culture. These special exhibitions add an extra layer of depth to the overall experience and provide visitors with fresh insights into Mozart's genius.

After exploring the birthplace, visitors can also visit the neighboring Mozart Residence, which was the family's home from 1773 to 1787. The residence offers further insights into Mozart's life and features a collection of original instruments, including his fortepiano. Together, the birthplace and residence provide a comprehensive overview of Mozart's life and work.

Salzburg Cathedral

Salzburg Cathedral, also known as Salzburger Dom, is a magnificent architectural masterpiece located in the heart of Salzburg, Austria. It is one of the most iconic landmarks in the city and a must-visit destination for travelers seeking to explore its rich history, stunning architecture, and religious significance.

Salzburg Cathedral is a Roman Catholic cathedral dedicated to Saint Rupert of Salzburg. It stands on the site of an early Christian church and has undergone several renovations and expansions over the centuries. The current structure dates back to the 17th century and showcases a blend of architectural styles, including Gothic, Renaissance, and Baroque elements.

The cathedral's exterior is characterized by its imposing facade adorned with intricate sculptures and reliefs. The main entrance features a grand portal with statues of the apostles and scenes from the life of Christ. Above the entrance, visitors can admire the magnificent rose window, which is a prominent feature of Gothic architecture.

Upon entering the cathedral, visitors are greeted by a breathtaking interior filled with ornate decorations, frescoes, and stunning artworks. The nave is adorned with beautiful stucco work and features grand arches that lead to side chapels. The high altar is a true masterpiece, showcasing intricate carvings and sculptures depicting biblical scenes.

One of the highlights of Salzburg Cathedral is its famous organ, which dates back to 1701. With over 4,000 pipes, it is one of the largest organs in Europe and is renowned for its exceptional sound quality. The cathedral regularly hosts organ concerts that attract music enthusiasts from around the world.

Another notable feature of Salzburg Cathedral is its crypt, which houses the tombs of several archbishops of Salzburg. The crypt provides a glimpse into the city's rich history and offers visitors an opportunity to pay their respects to these influential figures.

Aside from its architectural and historical significance, Salzburg Cathedral also plays an important role in religious life. It serves as the mother church of the Archdiocese of Salzburg and is a place of worship for locals and visitors alike. Masses are held regularly, and visitors are welcome to attend and experience the spiritual atmosphere of this sacred place.

Salzburg Cathedral is not only a place of worship but also a cultural hub. It hosts various events throughout the year, including concerts, choral performances, and religious ceremonies. One of the most famous events held at the cathedral is the annual Salzburg Festival, which showcases world-class music and theater performances.

While visiting Salzburg, a visit to Salzburg Cathedral is highly recommended. Its historical significance, architectural beauty, and cultural offerings make it a must-see attraction in the city. Whether you are interested in history, art, or spirituality, the cathedral offers something for everyone.

In addition to exploring the cathedral itself, visitors can also take advantage of its central location to explore other attractions in Salzburg. The cathedral is situated in the heart of the Old Town, a UNESCO World Heritage site known for its well-preserved medieval and baroque architecture. Nearby attractions include Mozart's Birthplace, Hohensalzburg Fortress, Mirabell Palace, and Gardens.

To fully appreciate the beauty and significance of Salzburg Cathedral, it is recommended to join a guided tour or hire an audio guide. These resources provide valuable insights into the history and architectural details of the cathedral, enhancing the overall visitor experience.

Hellbrunn Palace and Trick Fountains

Hellbrunn Palace and Trick Fountains in Salzburg is a popular destination for travelers seeking a unique and entertaining experience. Located just a few kilometers from the city center of Salzburg, Austria, Hellbrunn Palace offers visitors a glimpse into the extravagant lifestyle of the past while also providing an interactive and playful atmosphere through its famous trick fountains.

Hellbrunn Palace, also known as Schloss Hellbrunn, was built in the early 17th century by Prince-Archbishop Markus Sittikus von Hohenems. The palace was designed as a summer residence and pleasure palace, showcasing the wealth and power of the archbishops of Salzburg. It still survives as proof of their magnificence and richness today.

One of the main attractions at Hellbrunn Palace is its Trick Fountains. These fountains were designed to surprise and entertain guests with unexpected water features. The trick fountains are ingeniously hidden within the palace gardens, and visitors can explore them while taking guided tours. As visitors stroll through the gardens, they may encounter hidden water jets, grottos with water-powered figures, and even a dining table with water-spouting chairs.

The trick fountains at Hellbrunn Palace are not only visually stunning but also provide a refreshing respite during hot summer days. Visitors are advised to wear appropriate clothing as they may get wet while exploring the fountains. The playful nature of the trick fountains makes them a hit among both children and adults alike.

Aside from the trick fountains, Hellbrunn Palace offers other attractions that are worth exploring. The Palace Rooms provide a glimpse into the lavish lifestyle of the archbishops, with beautifully decorated halls, chambers, and salons showcasing exquisite furniture, artwork, and tapestries. Guided tours are available to provide historical context and insights into the palace's history.

The Hellbrunn Zoo is another highlight of the palace grounds. It is home to a variety of animals, including deer, peacocks, and various bird species. The zoo provides a serene and picturesque setting for visitors to enjoy nature and observe the animals in their natural habitats.

In addition to the main attractions, Hellbrunn Palace also hosts various cultural events and concerts throughout the year. These events range from classical music performances to theater productions, adding an extra layer of entertainment and cultural enrichment to the visitor experience.

When visiting Hellbrunn Palace and Trick Fountains, it is recommended to allocate at least half a day to fully explore the palace grounds and enjoy all the attractions it has to offer. The palace is easily accessible by public transportation or by car, with ample parking available on-site.

CHAPTER 6

Museums and Cultural Sites

Salzburg Museum

The Salzburg Museum, located in the city of Salzburg, Austria, is a must-visit destination for travelers interested in exploring the rich history and culture of the region. This comprehensive museum offers a wide range of exhibits and collections that showcase the art, history, and heritage of Salzburg and its surroundings.

The Salzburg Museum is situated in the Neue Residenz building, which itself holds historical significance as the former residence of the Prince-Archbishops of Salzburg. The museum was established in 2007 through the merger of several smaller museums in the city, with the aim of providing a unified and immersive experience for visitors.

The permanent exhibition "Salzburg. Story" is one of the attractions of the Salzburg Museum. This exhibition takes visitors on a journey through time, starting from the prehistoric era and leading up to the present day. Through a combination of artifacts, multimedia presentations, and interactive displays, visitors can gain a deep understanding of Salzburg's history, including its role as an important center for salt mining during Roman times and its development as a cultural hub under the rule of the Prince-Archbishops.

The museum also houses a remarkable collection of art, including paintings, sculptures, and decorative arts from various periods. The Salzburg Museum's art collection features works by renowned artists such as Wolfgang Amadeus Mozart's father Leopold Mozart and his sister Nannerl Mozart. These artworks provide insights into the artistic heritage of Salzburg and its influence on European art.

In addition to its permanent exhibitions, the Salzburg Museum regularly hosts temporary exhibitions that cover a wide range of topics related to art, history, and culture. These temporary exhibitions often feature collaborations with other museums and institutions, both nationally and internationally. This ensures that there is always something new and exciting to discover at the museum, making it an ideal destination for repeat visitors.

Furthermore, the Salzburg Museum offers various educational programs and activities for visitors of all ages. These include guided tours, workshops, and lectures that provide a deeper understanding of the museum's collections and exhibitions. The museum also has a dedicated children's area, where young visitors can engage in interactive and hands-on learning experiences.

The Salzburg Museum is not only a place for learning and exploration but also a venue for cultural events and performances.

The museum regularly hosts concerts, lectures, and other cultural activities that showcase the vibrant arts scene of Salzburg. These events provide visitors with an opportunity to experience the city's cultural heritage in a dynamic and engaging way.

Museum of Modern Art (Museum der Moderne)

The Museum of Modern Art (Museum der Moderne) in Salzburg is a must-visit destination for travelers interested in contemporary art and culture. Located on the Mönchsberg Mountain, the museum offers stunning panoramic views of the city while showcasing an impressive collection of modern and contemporary artworks.

The Museum of Modern Art in Salzburg is divided into two locations: the Rupertinum and the Mönchsberg. The Rupertinum, located in the heart of the old town, focuses on temporary exhibitions and special projects. It is housed in a historic building that was once a Franciscan monastery. The Mönchsberg location, on the other hand, is situated on top of the Mönchsberg Mountain and features a permanent collection as well as rotating exhibitions.

The permanent collection at the Museum of Modern Art in Salzburg includes works by renowned artists such as Pablo Picasso, Gustav Klimt, Egon Schiele, and Max Ernst. The museum's collection spans various artistic movements from the late 19th century to the present day, offering visitors a comprehensive overview of modern and contemporary art.

In addition to its permanent collection, the museum hosts temporary exhibitions that showcase works by both established and emerging artists. These exhibitions often explore current themes and trends in contemporary art, providing visitors with a dynamic and engaging experience.

One of the highlights of visiting the Museum of Modern Art in Salzburg is its unique location on the Mönchsberg Mountain. To reach the museum, visitors can take an elevator or walk up a scenic path that offers breathtaking views of the city along the way. Once inside, they can enjoy not only the artworks but also the panoramic windows that frame stunning vistas of Salzburg's historic center.

The museum also features a café with an outdoor terrace where visitors can relax and take in the beautiful surroundings. Additionally, there is a museum shop where art enthusiasts can purchase books, prints, and other art-related items.

If you are interested in learning more about the artworks on display, the Museum of Modern Art in Salzburg offers guided tours and educational programs. These activities provide deeper insights into the artists, their works, and the historical context in which they were created.

Mozart Residence Museum

The Mozart Residence Museum in Salzburg is a must-visit destination for travelers interested in the life and works of the renowned composer, Wolfgang Amadeus Mozart. Located in the heart of Salzburg's Old Town, this museum offers a unique opportunity to explore the living quarters of the Mozart family and gain insights into their daily lives.

The Mozart Residence Museum is situated at Makartplatz 8, which was once the residence of the Mozart family from 1773 to 1787. The museum showcases original artifacts, personal belongings, and memorabilia associated with Mozart and his family. It provides an immersive experience that allows visitors to step back in time and get a glimpse into the world of one of history's greatest musical geniuses.

Upon entering the museum, visitors are greeted with a comprehensive exhibition that spans three floors. The exhibition rooms are meticulously restored to reflect the ambiance of the late 18th century, providing an authentic atmosphere for visitors to immerse themselves in Mozart's world. The museum houses a vast collection of original instruments, including pianos, violins, and harpsichords that were owned and played by Mozart himself.

One of the highlights of the museum is the recreated living quarters of the Mozart family. Visitors can explore the rooms where Mozart composed some of his most famous works, including his childhood bedroom and his father Leopold's study. The rooms are furnished with period furniture and decor, giving visitors a sense of what life was like for the Mozarts during their time in Salzburg.

In addition to the living quarters, the museum also features an extensive collection of manuscripts, letters, and personal items belonging to Mozart and his family. These artifacts provide valuable insights into Mozart's creative process and personal life. Visitors can marvel at original compositions written by Mozart, read letters exchanged between him and his family members, and gain a deeper understanding of his musical genius.

The museum also offers audio guides in multiple languages, providing detailed commentary and explanations of the exhibits. These audio guides enhance the visitor experience by providing additional context and information about Mozart's life and works.

Aside from the permanent exhibition, the Mozart Residence Museum hosts temporary exhibitions that delve into various aspects of Mozart's life and music. These special exhibitions offer a fresh perspective on Mozart's legacy and provide visitors with an opportunity to explore different facets of his artistry.

The Mozart Residence Museum is not only a place for music enthusiasts but also for history buffs and culture seekers. It offers a comprehensive overview of Mozart's life, showcasing his impact on the musical world and his enduring legacy. The museum provides a unique opportunity to connect with the past and gain a deeper appreciation for one of history's most influential composers.

Visiting the Mozart Residence Museum is an enriching experience that allows travelers to immerse themselves in the world of Wolfgang Amadeus Mozart. Whether you are a fan of classical music or simply interested in history, this museum offers a captivating journey through the life and works of one of the greatest composers of all time.

DomQuartier Salzburg

The DomQuartier Salzburg is a must-visit destination for travelers in Salzburg, Austria. This historic complex is located in the heart of the city and offers a unique blend of architectural beauty, cultural heritage, and artistic treasures. It encompasses several prominent buildings, including the Salzburg Cathedral, the Residenz Palace, and the Benedictine St. Peter's Abbey.

The DomQuartier Salzburg holds immense historical significance as it was once the center of power for the Prince-Archbishops of Salzburg. It served as their residence and administrative headquarters, showcasing their wealth and influence.

One of the main attractions within the DomQuartier is the Salzburg Cathedral, also known as the Salzburger Dom. This magnificent Baroque-style cathedral is an architectural masterpiece that dates back to the 17th century. Its impressive facade, adorned with intricate sculptures and reliefs, captivates visitors from afar. Inside, the cathedral boasts stunning frescoes, ornate chapels, and a majestic organ that fills the space with heavenly music during concerts and religious services.

Adjacent to the cathedral is the Residenz Palace, which served as the official residence of the Prince-Archbishops. This opulent palace showcases various architectural styles ranging from late Gothic to Renaissance and Baroque. Visitors can explore its lavishly decorated rooms, including the state apartments, reception halls, and private chambers. The Residenz Gallery houses an extensive collection of European paintings from the 16th to 19th centuries, featuring works by renowned artists such as Rembrandt, Rubens, and Brueghel.

One of the oldest monasteries in Austria and another centerpiece of the DomQuartier is St. Peter's Abbey. Founded in 696 AD, this Benedictine abbey is steeped in history and spirituality. Its cemetery, with its elaborately designed tombstones, is the final resting place of many notable figures, including Mozart's sister

Nannerl. The abbey also houses a stunning library with a vast collection of ancient manuscripts and books.

Visitors to the DomQuartier can explore these remarkable buildings through a guided tour that takes them on a journey through Salzburg's rich cultural heritage. The tour provides insights into the history, art, and architecture of the complex, offering a comprehensive understanding of its significance. Additionally, visitors can enjoy panoramic views of Salzburg from the DomQuartier's observation terrace, which provides a breathtaking vista of the city's skyline.

In addition to its architectural and historical wonders, the DomQuartier hosts various cultural events throughout the year. These include classical music concerts, exhibitions, and special performances that showcase Salzburg's vibrant arts scene. The complex also features a charming café where visitors can relax and savor traditional Austrian delicacies while taking in the ambiance of this extraordinary setting.

CHAPTER 7

Outdoor Activities in Salzburg

Hiking and Nature Walks

Hiking and nature walks in Salzburg offer travelers a unique opportunity to explore the stunning natural beauty of the region. Salzburg, located in Austria, is known for its picturesque landscapes, majestic mountains, and charming alpine villages. Whether you are an avid hiker or simply enjoy leisurely walks surrounded by nature, Salzburg has something to offer for everyone.

One of the most popular hiking destinations in Salzburg is the Untersberg Mountain. Located just outside the city, this mountain offers a range of hiking trails suitable for all levels of experience. The Untersberg cable car takes visitors up to the summit, where they can enjoy breathtaking panoramic views of the surrounding area. From there, hikers have a variety of pathways to choose from that take them through lush forests, alpine meadows, and rocky terrain. The Almbach Gorge trail is particularly popular, as it takes hikers through a narrow gorge with cascading waterfalls and impressive rock formations.

Another must-visit hiking spot in Salzburg is the Hohe Tauern National Park. This park is the largest national park in Austria and is home to some of the country's highest peaks, including the Grossglockner, which stands at 3,798 meters (12,461 feet). The park provides a variety of hiking trails to suit people of all fitness levels and interests. From easy walks along crystal-clear mountain lakes to challenging multi-day treks through rugged terrain, there is something for everyone in Hohe Tauern National Park. Hikers can also spot a variety of wildlife in the park, including ibexes, chamois, and golden eagles.

For those looking for a more leisurely nature walk experience, Salzburg has several beautiful parks and gardens to explore. Mirabell Gardens, located in the heart of the city, is a UNESCO World Heritage Site and offers a peaceful oasis with manicured lawns, colorful flower beds, and ornamental fountains. The Hellbrunn Palace Gardens, another popular destination, feature a unique trick fountain system and are surrounded by lush greenery and walking paths. These gardens provide a tranquil setting for a relaxing stroll and are perfect for those who prefer a less strenuous outdoor activity.

When planning a hiking or nature walk in Salzburg, it is important to come prepared with the right gear and clothing. Comfortable hiking shoes, layered clothing, sunscreen, and a hat are essential items to bring along. It is also advisable to carry a map of the area and sufficient water and snacks to stay hydrated and energized during the hike.

In addition to the natural beauty, Salzburg also offers cultural and historical attractions that can be combined with hiking or nature walks. The city itself is renowned for its baroque architecture, including the iconic Hohensalzburg Fortress, which overlooks the city from atop Festungsberg hill. Visitors can take a leisurely walk up to the fortress or opt for a guided tour to learn more about its history. The Salzburg Zoo, located on Hellbrunn Mountain, is another popular attraction that can be easily accessed during a nature walk in the area.

Overall, hiking and nature walks in Salzburg provide travelers with an opportunity to immerse themselves in the stunning landscapes of Austria. Whether you choose to conquer mountain peaks or enjoy leisurely strolls through parks and gardens, Salzburg offers a diverse range of options for outdoor enthusiasts. So pack your hiking boots, grab your camera, and get ready to explore the natural wonders of Salzburg.

Cycling and Mountain Biking

Cycling and mountain biking in Salzburg offer travelers a unique and exhilarating way to explore the stunning landscapes and natural beauty of the region. With its diverse terrain, picturesque trails, and well-maintained cycling infrastructure, Salzburg is a paradise for cyclists of all levels. Whether you are a casual rider or an experienced mountain biker, there are plenty of options to suit your preferences and abilities.

Salzburg's Cycling Infrastructure:

Salzburg boasts an extensive network of cycling paths and routes that cater to both leisurely cyclists and avid mountain bikers. The city is committed to promoting cycling as a sustainable mode of transportation and has invested in developing a comprehensive cycling infrastructure. This includes dedicated bike lanes, well-marked cycling routes, and bike-friendly facilities such as parking areas and repair stations.

Cycling Routes in Salzburg:

Tauern Cycle Path: One of the most popular cycling routes in Salzburg is the Tauern Cycle Path. This scenic route stretches for approximately 270 kilometers (168 miles) from Krimml in the Hohe Tauern National Park to Passau in Germany. The path follows the Salzach River, offering breathtaking views of the surrounding mountains, charming villages, and historical landmarks along the way.

Lake Wolfgang Cycle Path: For those seeking a more leisurely ride, the Lake Wolfgang Cycle Path is an excellent choice. This

10-kilometer (6-mile) route circles Lake Wolfgang, one of Austria's most picturesque lakes. Cyclists can enjoy stunning views of the lake and its surrounding mountains while passing through quaint villages like St. Gilgen and Strobl.

Gaisberg Mountain Bike Park: Mountain biking enthusiasts will find plenty of thrilling trails at Gaisberg Mountain Bike Park. Located just outside Salzburg, this park offers a variety of trails suitable for different skill levels. From gentle forest paths to challenging downhill tracks, riders can experience the adrenaline rush of mountain biking while enjoying panoramic views of the city and the Alps.

Mountain Biking in Salzburg:

Salzburg's mountainous terrain provides ample opportunities for mountain biking enthusiasts to test their skills and explore the region's natural wonders. The surrounding mountains offer a wide range of trails, from gentle slopes for beginners to steep and technical descents for advanced riders. Some popular mountain biking destinations near Salzburg include:

Saalbach-Hinterglemm: Located approximately 90 kilometers (56 miles) southwest of Salzburg, Saalbach-Hinterglemm is a renowned mountain biking destination. The area features over 400 kilometers (250 miles) of marked trails, including downhill tracks, cross-country routes, and freeride options. With its stunning alpine scenery and well-maintained trails, Saalbach-Hinterglemm attracts mountain bikers from around the world.

Leogang Bike Park: Situated in the same region as Saalbach-Hinterglemm, Leogang Bike Park is a must-visit destination for downhill and freeride enthusiasts. The park offers a variety of trails with different difficulty levels, including the famous "Speedster" downhill track used for international competitions. Riders can also take advantage of the park's lift system, which allows for multiple runs without exhausting climbs.

Dachstein-Tauern Region: Located southeast of Salzburg, the Dachstein-Tauern region offers breathtaking mountain biking opportunities. The area features a vast network of trails that traverse through alpine meadows, dense forests, and rugged peaks. Cyclists can explore the picturesque villages of Ramsau am Dachstein and Schladming while enjoying panoramic views of the Dachstein Glacier and surrounding mountains.

Cycling Tours and Services:

For travelers who prefer guided tours or require bike rentals and support services, there are several reputable companies in Salzburg that cater to cyclists. These companies offer a range of services, including guided cycling tours, bike rentals, equipment sales, and maintenance. They can provide valuable local knowledge, ensuring that cyclists make the most of their time in Salzburg and discover hidden gems along the way.

Water Sports on the Salzach River

Water sports on the Salzach River in Salzburg offer travelers a unique and thrilling experience. The Salzach River, flowing through the picturesque city of Salzburg, provides a stunning backdrop for various water activities. Whether you are seeking adrenaline-pumping adventures or a leisurely day on the water, there are plenty of options to cater to all interests and skill levels.

Rafting is one of the most popular water sports on the Salzach River. It offers an exciting and exhilarating experience as you navigate through the river's rapids and waves. Rafting trips are available for both beginners and experienced rafters, with different routes and difficulty levels to choose from. Professional guides accompany each trip to ensure safety and provide instructions on paddling techniques.

Kayaking is another thrilling water sport that allows travelers to explore the Salzach River at their own pace. With its calm sections and occasional rapids, the river offers an ideal setting for kayaking enthusiasts. Renting a kayak or joining a guided tour provides an opportunity to enjoy the scenic beauty of Salzburg while engaging in an active adventure.

For those seeking a more relaxed experience, stand-up paddleboarding (SUP) is a fantastic option. SUP involves standing on a large board and using a paddle to navigate through the water. It is a great way to enjoy the tranquility of the Salzach River while also engaging in a full-body workout. SUP rentals are available along the riverbanks, allowing travelers to explore at their own pace.

In addition to these popular water sports, there are other activities available on the Salzach River that cater to different interests. Canoeing provides a peaceful way to explore the river's natural surroundings, allowing travelers to immerse themselves in nature while gliding along the water. River surfing is also gaining popularity in Salzburg, particularly near the city's famous Makartsteg Bridge. This unique sport involves riding the river's standing waves on a surfboard, providing an adrenaline rush for experienced surfers.

When planning to engage in water sports on the Salzach River, it is essential to prioritize safety. Always wear appropriate safety gear, such as life jackets and helmets, and follow the instructions provided by professional guides. It is also advisable to check weather conditions and water levels before embarking on any water activities.

Travelers visiting Salzburg can easily find reputable companies that offer water sports experiences on the Salzach River. These companies provide equipment rentals, guided tours, and expert instruction to ensure a safe and enjoyable experience for all participants. It is recommended to book in advance, especially during peak tourist seasons, to secure your preferred time slot.

In conclusion, water sports on the Salzach River in Salzburg offer travelers a thrilling and memorable experience. Whether you choose rafting, kayaking, stand-up paddleboarding, canoeing, or river surfing, there are options available for all skill levels and preferences. Enjoy the stunning scenery of Salzburg while engaging in these exciting activities that will undoubtedly add an extra element of adventure to your trip.

CHAPTER 8

Shopping in Salzburg

Getreidegasse

Getreidegasse is a renowned shopping street located in the heart of Salzburg, Austria. It is known for its charming atmosphere, historic buildings, and a wide range of shops offering unique and high-quality products. Whether you are a local resident or a traveler visiting Salzburg, exploring the shops in Getreidegasse is an experience not to be missed.

Traditional Austrian Products:

One of the highlights of shopping in Getreidegasse is the opportunity to discover and purchase traditional Austrian products. The street is lined with shops that specialize in selling authentic Austrian goods such as clothing, accessories, crafts, and souvenirs. These products often showcase the rich cultural heritage of Austria and make for excellent keepsakes or gifts.

Fashion and Luxury Brands:

Getreidegasse is also home to a variety of fashion boutiques and luxury brand stores. International fashion labels, as well as local designers, have set up shop in this iconic street. Visitors can find a wide range of clothing, shoes, accessories, and jewelry from renowned brands. Whether you are looking for high-end designer pieces or trendy fashion items, Getreidegasse offers a diverse selection to cater to different tastes and budgets.

Specialty Stores:

In addition to traditional Austrian products and fashion brands, Getreidegasse boasts several specialty stores that cater to specific interests and hobbies. These stores offer unique items related to music, art supplies, books, antiques, and more. Music enthusiasts can explore shops dedicated to classical music recordings or musical instruments. Art lovers can find galleries showcasing local artists' works or stores selling art supplies for their own creative endeavors.

Souvenirs and Gifts:

For travelers looking to bring back souvenirs or gifts from their visit to Salzburg, Getreidegasse is the perfect place to shop. The street is filled with shops offering a wide range of souvenirs, including traditional Austrian trinkets, postcards, magnets, and more. These items serve as reminders of your time in Salzburg and make for meaningful gifts for friends and family back home.

Culinary Delights:

Getreidegasse is not just about shopping for material goods; it also offers a delightful culinary experience. The street is dotted with cafes, bakeries, and specialty food stores where visitors can indulge in delicious Austrian pastries, chocolates, cheeses, and other local delicacies. Exploring the culinary offerings of Getreidegasse adds another layer of enjoyment to your shopping experience.

Architectural Beauty:

Apart from the shopping opportunities, Getreidegasse itself is a sight to behold. The street is famous for its well-preserved medieval architecture, featuring colorful facades, ornate signs, and wrought-iron guild signs. As you stroll along the cobblestone streets, take a moment to appreciate the unique architectural details that add to the charm of this historic shopping destination.

Mozart's Birthplace:

While exploring Getreidegasse, don't miss the chance to visit Mozart's Birthplace. Located at No. 9 Getreidegasse, this museum provides insight into the life and works of one of the world's greatest composers, Wolfgang Amadeus Mozart. The museum also houses a gift shop where you can find music-related souvenirs and memorabilia.

In conclusion, shopping in Getreidegasse, Salzburg offers a diverse and enriching experience for travelers. From traditional Austrian products to fashion brands, specialty stores to culinary delights, there is something for everyone in this historic shopping street. The combination of unique shops, architectural beauty, and cultural significance makes Getreidegasse a must-visit destination for any traveler in Salzburg.

Linzergasse

Linzergasse is a charming and historic street located in the heart of Salzburg, Austria. It is known for its picturesque architecture, vibrant atmosphere, and a wide range of shops that cater to both locals and tourists. Whether you are looking for unique souvenirs, fashionable clothing, or delicious local delicacies, Linzergasse has something to offer for everyone. Let's explore the various shopping options available in Linzergasse and provide valuable information for travelers.

Souvenirs and Gifts:

Linzergasse is a haven for souvenir hunters, with numerous shops offering a wide variety of traditional Austrian gifts and mementos. Visitors can find beautifully crafted wooden toys, hand-painted ceramics, intricate glassware, and traditional clothing such as dirndls and lederhosen. One popular store is "Salzburg Souvenir Shop," which offers an extensive selection of high-quality souvenirs that reflect the rich cultural heritage of Salzburg. Another notable shop is "Austria Shop," where you can find a range of authentic Austrian products including Mozart chocolates, music boxes, and Alpine-themed accessories.

Fashion and Accessories:

Fashion enthusiasts will not be disappointed when exploring the fashion boutiques along Linzergasse. The street is lined with trendy clothing stores that showcase both local designers and international brands. "Modehaus Lanz" is a renowned fashion boutique that offers a curated collection of stylish clothing for men and women. They specialize in traditional Austrian attire with a modern twist. For those seeking luxury brands, "Linzergasse Fashion" is a must-visit store that features high-end designer labels from around the world.

In addition to clothing, Linzergasse also offers a wide range of accessories to complement your style. "Schmuckstücke" is a jewelry store that showcases unique and handcrafted pieces made by local artisans. From delicate silver earrings to statement necklaces, this store has something for every taste. For those interested in eyewear, "Optik Linzergasse" provides a wide selection of designer glasses and sunglasses.

Food and Delicacies:

Linzergasse is not only a paradise for shoppers but also a culinary delight. The street is home to several specialty food stores where you can find delicious local delicacies and gourmet treats. "Käsehaus" is a cheese lover's dream, offering an extensive selection of Austrian cheeses, including the famous Salzburg Mozartkugel cheese. "Salzburger Nockerl" is another popular store that specializes in traditional Austrian pastries, such as the iconic Salzburger Nockerl dessert.

For chocolate lovers, "Zotter Schokoladen Manufaktur" is a must-visit destination. This renowned chocolate factory offers a wide range of organic and fair-trade chocolates with unique flavors and creative combinations. Visitors can take guided tours to learn about the chocolate-making process and indulge in tasting sessions.

Conclusion:

Shopping in Linzergasse, Salzburg, offers a delightful experience for travelers. From traditional souvenirs to fashionable clothing and mouthwatering delicacies, this historic street has something for everyone. Whether you are looking to immerse yourself in Austrian culture or simply enjoy a leisurely shopping spree, Linzergasse is the perfect destination.

Europark Shopping Center

Europark Shopping Center is one of the largest and most popular shopping destinations in Salzburg, Austria. Located just a few kilometers from the city center, Europark offers a wide range of shopping options for both locals and tourists alike.

Overview of Europark Shopping Center:

Europark Shopping Center is a modern and spacious mall that covers an area of over 36,000 square meters. It first opened its doors in 1990 and has since become a favorite shopping destination for both residents and visitors to Salzburg. The mall features a unique architectural design with an open-air concept, allowing shoppers to enjoy natural light while exploring the various stores.

Stores and Brands:

Europark offers a diverse range of stores, catering to different tastes and preferences. From high-end luxury brands to affordable fashion retailers, there is something for everyone at this shopping center. Some of the popular international brands found at Europark include Zara, H&M, Mango, Esprit, and Swarovski. Additionally, there are several local Austrian brands that offer unique products and souvenirs.

Fashion and Apparel:

Fashion enthusiasts will be delighted by the extensive selection of clothing stores at Europark. Whether you are looking for trendy outfits or timeless classics, you will find a wide range of options to choose from. The mall houses multiple fashion retailers offering men's, women's, and children's clothing, as well as accessories such as shoes, bags, and jewelry.

Electronics and Technology:

For tech-savvy travelers, Europark has several stores dedicated to electronics and technology products. From smartphones and laptops to cameras and gaming consoles, you can find all the latest gadgets at competitive prices. Popular electronics retailers at Europark include Media Markt and Saturn, known for their wide selection and knowledgeable staff.

Home and Decor:

If you are looking to spruce up your living space or find unique home decor items, Europark has a variety of stores that cater to these needs. From furniture and kitchenware to decorative accessories and bedding, you will find everything you need to create a stylish and comfortable home environment.

Food and Dining:

After a long day of shopping, visitors can indulge in a wide range of culinary delights at Europark's food court or one of the many restaurants scattered throughout the mall. The food court offers a diverse selection of international cuisines, including Asian, Italian, and traditional Austrian dishes. Whether you are craving a quick snack or a full meal, there are plenty of options to satisfy your taste buds.

Services and Amenities:

Europark Shopping Center provides various services and amenities to enhance the shopping experience for visitors. These include free Wi-Fi throughout the mall, baby changing facilities, wheelchair accessibility, and ample parking spaces. Additionally, there are information desks located at strategic points within the mall where friendly staff members can assist with any inquiries or provide directions.

Events and Entertainment:

Europark regularly hosts events and activities to engage shoppers and create a vibrant atmosphere. These events may include fashion shows, live performances, product launches, or seasonal celebrations. Travelers should check the mall's website or social media channels for updates on upcoming events during their visit.

Location and Transportation:

Europark Shopping Center is conveniently located just outside Salzburg's city center, making it easily accessible for travelers. The address is Europastraße 1, 5018 Salzburg, Austria. Visitors can reach Europark by car via the A1 motorway or by public transportation using bus lines 1, 2, 10, or 27. The mall also offers ample parking spaces for those who prefer to drive.

Opening Hours:

Europark is open from Monday to Friday, typically from 9:00 am to 7:00 pm. On Saturdays, the mall opens at 9:00 am and closes at 6:00 pm. Some stores may have slightly different opening hours, so it is advisable to check the individual store's schedule before planning your visit.

In conclusion, Europark Shopping Center in Salzburg offers a diverse and enjoyable shopping experience for travelers. With its wide range of stores, including fashion, electronics, home decor, and dining options, visitors can find everything they need in one convenient location. The mall's services, amenities, and regular events further enhance the overall experience. Whether you are a fashion enthusiast, tech-savvy traveler, or simply looking for a place to relax and enjoy good food, Europark has something for everyone.

CHAPTER 9

Dining and Cuisine

Restaurants in Salzburg

As a popular tourist destination, Salzburg offers a wide range of dining options to cater to the diverse tastes of travelers. From traditional Austrian cuisine to international flavors, there are numerous restaurants in Salzburg that provide delightful culinary experiences. Here are some notable restaurants in Salzburg along with their locations and food prices:

Stiftskeller St. Peter: Located in the heart of Salzburg's Old Town, Stiftskeller St. Peter is one of the oldest restaurants in Europe, dating back to 803 AD. This historic establishment offers a unique dining experience in a charming setting. The menu features traditional Austrian dishes such as Wiener Schnitzel, Tafelspitz (boiled beef), and Salzburger Nockerl (a sweet soufflé). Prices at Stiftskeller St. Peter range from €20 to €40 for main courses.

Restaurant Ikarus: Situated within Hangar-7 at Salzburg Airport, Restaurant Ikarus is a culinary hotspot known for its innovative concept. Every month, a different guest chef from around the world takes over the kitchen, creating an ever-changing menu that showcases their signature dishes. This restaurant offers a truly unique gastronomic experience with prices ranging from €80 to €150 per person.

M32: Perched atop the Museum der Moderne on Mönchsberg Mountain, M32 offers breathtaking panoramic views of Salzburg's skyline while serving contemporary Austrian cuisine. The menu includes dishes like roasted venison, trout fillet, and pumpkin risotto. Prices at M32 vary from €25 to €45 for main courses.

Triangel: Located near Mirabell Palace and Gardens, Triangel is a cozy restaurant that specializes in traditional Austrian fare with a modern twist. The menu features dishes like beef goulash, roasted duck, and Kaiserschmarrn (shredded pancake dessert). Prices at Triangel range from €15 to €30 for main courses.

Zum Zirkelwirt: Situated in the historic district of Salzburg, Zum Zirkelwirt is a family-run restaurant that offers a warm and welcoming atmosphere. The menu focuses on regional specialties such as Kasnocken (cheese dumplings), Schweinsbraten (roast pork), and Apfelstrudel (apple strudel). Prices at Zum Zirkelwirt range from €15 to €25 for main courses.

S'Herzl: Located in the Altstadt neighborhood, S'Herzl is a popular restaurant known for its modern Austrian cuisine. The menu features dishes made with locally sourced ingredients, including veal medallions, grilled trout, and spinach dumplings. Prices at S'Herzl vary from €20 to €40 for main courses.

PitterKeller: Situated in the basement of Hotel IMLAUER & Bräu, PitterKeller is a traditional beer cellar that offers hearty Austrian dishes and a wide selection of beers. The menu includes classics like Wiener Schnitzel, pork knuckle, and sausage platters. Prices at PitterKeller range from €15 to €30 for main courses.

Augustiner Bräustübl: Located near the Müllner Steintor Bridge, Augustiner Bräustübl is a popular beer hall that serves traditional Austrian food alongside its own brewed beer. Visitors can enjoy dishes like roasted pork, sausages, and pretzels while savoring the lively atmosphere. Prices at Augustiner Bräustübl range from €10 to €20 for main courses.

It is important to note that the prices mentioned above are approximate and can vary depending on the specific dish, season, and any additional services or extras included in the dining experience. Additionally, it is advisable to make reservations in advance, especially during peak tourist seasons, to secure a table at these popular restaurants.

Traditional Austrian Dishes

Traditional Austrian cuisine is known for its rich flavors, hearty portions, and diverse range of dishes. For travelers visiting Austria, exploring the local culinary scene is a must-do experience. From savory meat dishes to delectable pastries, here are some traditional Austrian dishes that you should try during your visit, along with their locations and approximate food prices.

Wiener Schnitzel:

Wiener Schnitzel is perhaps the most famous Austrian dish worldwide. It consists of a breaded and fried veal cutlet, traditionally served with a slice of lemon and potato salad or parsley potatoes. This iconic dish can be found in many restaurants across Austria, particularly in Vienna, where it originated. The price of a Wiener Schnitzel can vary depending on the restaurant and location, but it typically ranges from €10 to €20.

Tafelspitz:

Tafelspitz is a classic Austrian beef dish that is often considered the national dish of Austria. It consists of boiled beef simmered with root vegetables and spices, resulting in tender and flavorful meat. Tafelspitz is typically served with traditional side dishes such as apple horseradish sauce, chive sauce, roasted potatoes, and creamed spinach. You can find this dish in many traditional Viennese restaurants, as well as in other regions of Austria. The price for Tafelspitz can range from €15 to €30.

Käsespätzle:

Käsespätzle is a popular Austrian comfort food that originated in the Alpine regions. It is a dish made of soft egg noodles mixed with melted cheese (usually Emmental or Gruyère) and topped with crispy fried onions. Käsespätzle is often served as a main course or as a side dish to accompany meat dishes such as roasted pork or sausages. You can find this dish in traditional Austrian restaurants, especially in the mountainous regions of Tyrol and Salzburg. The price for Käsespätzle can range from €8 to €15.

Sachertorte:

No visit to Austria would be complete without trying the famous Sachertorte. This indulgent chocolate cake is a Viennese specialty and has become a symbol of Austrian cuisine. It consists of two layers of dense chocolate cake filled with apricot jam and covered in a smooth chocolate glaze. Sachertorte is often served with whipped cream on the side. You can enjoy this delicious dessert in many Viennese coffee houses, as well as in pastry shops throughout Austria. The price for a slice of Sachertorte can range from €4 to €8.

Apfelstrudel:

Apfelstrudel, or apple strudel, is another beloved Austrian dessert that shouldn't be missed. It is made of thin layers of flaky pastry filled with spiced apples, raisins, and breadcrumbs. The strudel is then baked until golden brown and served warm, often accompanied by vanilla sauce or a scoop of vanilla ice cream. Apfelstrudel can be found in many traditional Austrian bakeries, cafes, and restaurants across the country. The price for a slice of Apfelstrudel can range from €3 to €6.

It's important to note that food prices mentioned above are approximate and can vary depending on the restaurant's location, level of service, and other factors. Additionally, these dishes are just a small sample of the wide variety of traditional Austrian cuisine available throughout the country.

Local Salzburg Specialties

Salzburg is known for its rich culinary traditions and local specialties that are a must-try for travelers. From hearty dishes to sweet treats, the city offers a wide range of options to satisfy every palate. Let's explore some of the top local Salzburg specialties, along with their locations and approximate food prices.

Schnitzel: Schnitzel is a classic Austrian dish that has become popular worldwide. It consists of a breaded and fried meat cutlet, typically made from veal or pork. In Salzburg, you can find excellent schnitzel at various traditional Austrian restaurants and gasthofs (inns). One highly recommended place is Gasthof Goldgasse, located in the heart of Salzburg's old town. The price for a schnitzel dish at Gasthof Goldgasse ranges from €15 to €25 ($18 to $30).

Salzburger Nockerl: Salzburger Nockerl is a famous sweet soufflé dessert that originated in Salzburg. It is made from egg whites, sugar, and vanilla, baked until it forms a light and fluffy texture. This delightful treat is often served with powdered sugar sprinkled on top. To taste authentic Salzburger Nockerl, head to Café Tomaselli, one of the oldest coffee houses in Salzburg. The price for a serving of Salzburger Nockerl at Café Tomaselli is around €8 to €10 ($9 to $12).

Mozartkugel: Mozartkugel is a beloved chocolate treat named after the famous composer Wolfgang Amadeus Mozart, who was born in Salzburg. It consists of a marzipan core surrounded by nougat and coated with dark chocolate. The original Mozartkugel can be found at Café-Konditorei Fürst, which claims to have invented this delicacy. Located in the heart of Salzburg's old town, a single Mozartkugel at Café-Konditorei Fürst costs approximately €1.50 ($1.80).

Kasnocken: Kasnocken is a traditional Austrian cheese dumpling dish that is popular in Salzburg. It is made by mixing flour, eggs, and grated cheese, then boiling the mixture until it forms dumplings. The dumplings are typically served with melted butter and sprinkled with chives. One great place to try Kasnocken in

Salzburg is Gasthaus Zwettler's Stiftskeller, located near the Salzburg Cathedral. The price for a plate of Kasnocken at Gasthaus Zwettler's Stiftskeller ranges from €10 to €15 ($12 to $18).

Brettljause: Brettljause is a traditional Austrian snack platter that consists of various cold cuts, cheeses, pickles, and bread. It is perfect for sharing and experiencing a variety of flavors in one sitting. In Salzburg, you can enjoy a delicious Brettljause at Augustiner Bräustübl, a historic beer hall and garden. The price for a Brettljause platter at Augustiner Bräustübl starts at around €10 ($12) per person.

Salzburger Bier: While not a specific food item, Salzburg is also known for its excellent local beers. The city has several breweries that produce a wide range of beer styles, including lagers, wheat beers, and specialty brews. One popular brewery in Salzburg is Stiegl Brewery, which offers guided tours and tastings for beer enthusiasts. The price for a pint of Salzburger beer at local pubs and breweries varies but generally ranges from €3 to €5 ($3.60 to $6).

These are just a few examples of the local specialties that Salzburg has to offer. Exploring the city's culinary scene will undoubtedly provide travelers with a memorable and delicious experience.

International Cuisine Options

Let's explore some of the top international cuisine options in Salzburg, along with their locations and food prices.

Taj Mahal Indian Restaurant

Location: Rudolfskai 8, 5020 Salzburg

Food Prices: The average price for a main course at Taj Mahal Indian Restaurant ranges from €10 to €20.

Taj Mahal Indian Restaurant is a highly regarded establishment that brings the flavors of India to Salzburg. Located in the heart of the city, this restaurant offers an extensive menu featuring authentic Indian dishes prepared with fresh ingredients and aromatic spices. From classic curries to tandoori specialties and vegetarian options, Taj Mahal provides a diverse range of choices for both meat lovers and vegetarians alike. The restaurant's warm ambiance and attentive service add to the overall dining experience.

Ikarus Restaurant

Location: Hangar-7, Wilhelm-Spazier-Straße 7A, 5020 Salzburg

Food Prices: The price for a multi-course menu at Ikarus Restaurant starts at €145 per person.

Ikarus Restaurant is an exceptional dining establishment located within Hangar-7, an impressive aviation museum in Salzburg. What sets Ikarus apart is its unique concept of inviting renowned international guest chefs who create exclusive menus for a limited time period. Each month, a different chef from around the world takes over the kitchen, showcasing their culinary expertise and signature dishes. This innovative approach allows visitors to experience a variety of international cuisines without leaving Salzburg.

Zum Zirkelwirt Italian Restaurant

Location: Linzer Gasse 47, 5020 Salzburg

Food Prices: The average price for a main course at Zum Zirkelwirt Italian Restaurant ranges from €10 to €20.

Zum Zirkelwirt is a charming Italian restaurant situated in the historic district of Salzburg. With its cozy atmosphere and friendly staff, it offers a delightful dining experience for lovers of Italian cuisine. The menu features a wide selection of traditional Italian dishes, including pasta, risotto, pizza, and seafood specialties. The restaurant prides itself on using high-quality ingredients sourced both locally and from Italy to ensure an authentic taste.

S'Kloane Brauhaus

Location: Giselakai 3-5, 5020 Salzburg

Food Prices: The average price for a main course at S'Kloane Brauhaus ranges from €10 to €20.

S'Kloane Brauhaus is a popular spot for those seeking hearty Austrian and Bavarian dishes in Salzburg. Located near the Salzach River, this traditional brewery and restaurant offers a cozy setting with rustic decor. The menu includes classic Austrian dishes such as Wiener Schnitzel, Tafelspitz (boiled beef), and various sausages. Visitors can also enjoy a selection of locally brewed beers to complement their meal.

El Pescador Seafood Restaurant

Location: Gstättengasse 13, 5020 Salzburg

Food Prices: The average price for a main course at El Pescador Seafood Restaurant ranges from €15 to €30.

El Pescador Seafood Restaurant brings the flavors of the sea to Salzburg. Situated in the city center, this restaurant specializes in fresh seafood dishes prepared with Mediterranean influences. From grilled fish and seafood platters to paella and seafood pasta, El Pescador offers a diverse range of options for seafood enthusiasts.

The restaurant's cozy interior and attentive service create a welcoming atmosphere for diners.

These are just a few examples of the international cuisine options available in Salzburg. Whether you're craving Indian, Italian, Austrian, or seafood delights, the city has something to offer for every palate. It's worth noting that prices mentioned above are approximate and can vary depending on the specific dish and restaurant.

CHAPTER 10

Nightlife and Entertainment

Bars and Pubs

As a traveler looking to experience the local nightlife and enjoy a drink or two, Salzburg offers a variety of bars and pubs that cater to different tastes and preferences. Here are some notable establishments in Salzburg along with their locations:

Augustiner Bräu - Located at Lindhofstraße 7, Augustiner Bräu is one of the most famous beer halls in Salzburg. Housed in a former monastery, this traditional beer garden offers a unique atmosphere where visitors can enjoy locally brewed beer straight from wooden barrels. The venue also features a self-service system where patrons can bring their own food or purchase traditional Austrian dishes from various stalls.

Shamrock Irish Pub - Situated at Rudolfskai 12, Shamrock Irish Pub is a popular spot for both locals and tourists seeking an authentic Irish pub experience. With its cozy interior, live music performances, and a wide selection of Irish whiskeys and beers, this pub provides a warm and welcoming atmosphere. Additionally, they often broadcast major sporting events on large screens, making it an ideal place for sports enthusiasts.

Die Weisse - Found at Rupertgasse 10, Die Weisse is a charming brewery and beer garden that has been serving its own craft beer since 1901. This family-owned establishment offers a range of traditional Austrian dishes alongside their signature brews. The outdoor seating area provides a relaxed setting where visitors can enjoy their drinks while taking in the picturesque views of the surrounding mountains.

O'Malley's Irish Pub - Located at Rudolfskai 8, O'Malley's Irish Pub is another well-known establishment in Salzburg that captures the essence of an authentic Irish pub. With its rustic interior, friendly staff, and live music performances, this pub creates a lively and enjoyable atmosphere. They offer a wide selection of Irish beers, whiskeys, and pub food, making it a popular choice among locals and tourists alike.

The Old Irish Pub - Situated at Gstättengasse 19, The Old Irish Pub is a cozy and intimate venue that provides an authentic Irish pub experience in the heart of Salzburg. Known for its friendly staff and warm ambiance, this pub offers a wide range of Irish beers, spirits, and cocktails. Live music performances are also a regular feature here, adding to the overall lively atmosphere.

Bärenwirt - Found at Müllner Hauptstraße 8, Bärenwirt is a historic tavern that has been serving customers since 1663. This traditional Austrian establishment offers a rustic setting with wooden interiors and serves a variety of local beers and traditional dishes. With its long-standing history and charming atmosphere, Bärenwirt provides visitors with an authentic taste of Salzburg's culinary heritage.

These are just a few examples of the many bars and pubs available in Salzburg for travelers to explore. Each establishment offers its own unique atmosphere, drink selection, and cultural experience, ensuring that there is something for everyone to enjoy during their visit to this beautiful city.

Music and Concert Venues

Salzburg offers a variety of music venues that cater to different tastes and preferences. From classical concerts to contemporary performances, Salzburg has something to offer every music enthusiast. Here are some of the notable music and concert venues in Salzburg, along with their locations:

Mozarteum University: Located in the heart of Salzburg's historic center, Mozarteum University is a prestigious institution dedicated to music and performing arts education. The university hosts numerous concerts throughout the year, featuring talented students, faculty members, and guest artists. The main concert hall, known as the Mozarteum Großer Saal, is an elegant venue with excellent acoustics.

Salzburg Festival: The Salzburg Festival is one of the most renowned classical music festivals in the world. It takes place annually during the summer months and attracts top musicians, conductors, and opera singers from around the globe. The festival utilizes several venues across the city, including the iconic Grosses Festspielhaus (Large Festival Hall), Haus für Mozart (House for Mozart), and Felsenreitschule (Rock Riding School). These venues are located within walking distance of each other in Salzburg's historic district.

Mirabell Palace and Gardens: Mirabell Palace, a UNESCO World Heritage Site, is not only famous for its stunning architecture and beautiful gardens but also for its musical heritage. The palace features a grand marble hall known as the Marble Hall (Marmorsaal), which serves as a venue for chamber music concerts and recitals. Located on Mirabellplatz in the city center, this venue offers an intimate setting for enjoying classical music performances.

Salzburg Congress: Situated near Mirabell Palace, Salzburg Congress is a modern conference center that also hosts various cultural events, including concerts. The center's main hall, the Salzburg Congress Saal, is a versatile space that can accommodate large-scale concerts and performances. It is equipped with state-of-the-art audiovisual technology and offers excellent acoustics.

St. Peter's Abbey: St. Peter's Abbey, one of the oldest monasteries in Austria, is not only a historic landmark but also a venue for classical music concerts. The abbey's Stiftskeller St. Peter restaurant hosts regular Mozart dinner concerts, where visitors can enjoy a traditional Austrian meal accompanied by live performances of Mozart's music. The abbey is located in the Altstadt (Old Town) area of Salzburg.

Salzburg Marionette Theatre: For those interested in a unique musical experience, the Salzburg Marionette Theatre offers puppetry performances set to classical music. Located at Schwarzstraße 24, near the Mirabell Gardens, this theater has been entertaining audiences since 1913 with its enchanting marionette shows.

Rockhouse Salzburg: If you're looking for a more contemporary music scene, Rockhouse Salzburg is a popular venue for live rock, pop, and alternative music concerts. Located at Schallmooser Hauptstraße 46, this vibrant club hosts both local and international bands and artists.

Jazzit: Jazzit is a renowned jazz club in Salzburg that showcases live jazz performances from local and international musicians. Located at Elisabethstraße 11a, near the city center, Jazzit offers an intimate setting for enjoying the improvisational sounds of jazz.

These are just a few examples of the diverse music and concert venues available in Salzburg for travelers to explore and enjoy during their visit.

Festivals and Events

As a Traveler visiting Salzburg, You can immerse yourself in the city's lively atmosphere by attending various festivals and events throughout the year. From classical music concerts to traditional folk festivals, Salzburg offers a diverse range of experiences for travelers to enjoy. Here are some of the most popular festivals and events in Salzburg.

Salzburg Festival:

The Salzburg Festival is undoubtedly the most famous and prestigious event in the city. Established in 1920, it is a celebration of music and performing arts that attracts visitors from all over the world. Held annually during the summer months, the festival showcases a wide range of performances including opera, theater, orchestral concerts, and chamber music. The festival takes place at various iconic venues in Salzburg, such as the Salzburg Festival Hall, Mozarteum University, and Felsenreitschule. Renowned artists and ensembles from around the globe come together to present exceptional performances, making it a must-visit event for any traveler interested in classical music and performing arts.

Mozart Week:

Salzburg is famously known as the birthplace of Wolfgang Amadeus Mozart, one of the greatest composers in history. To honor his legacy, the city hosts an annual Mozart Week festival. Taking place in late January or early February, this festival celebrates Mozart's music through a series of concerts and performances held at various venues across Salzburg. The festival features renowned orchestras, soloists, and chamber ensembles interpreting Mozart's compositions with exceptional skill and artistry. Travelers can indulge in the beauty of Mozart's music while exploring the city's historical sites associated with his life.

Salzburg Advent Singing:

For travelers visiting Salzburg during the Christmas season, the Salzburg Advent Singing is a magical event not to be missed. Held in the Salzburg Arena, this traditional folk festival brings together choirs, musicians, and dancers to perform enchanting Christmas carols and folk songs. The festival showcases the rich cultural heritage of the region, with participants dressed in traditional costumes and performing age-old customs. Visitors can experience the festive spirit of Salzburg while enjoying the heartwarming melodies and witnessing the vibrant traditions of the local community.

Salzburg Easter Festival:

The Salzburg Easter Festival is another prominent event that attracts music enthusiasts from around the world. Founded by Herbert von Karajan, one of the most influential conductors of the 20th century, this festival focuses on presenting exceptional opera and orchestral performances during the Easter season. Renowned opera houses and orchestras collaborate to bring masterpieces to life on stage, creating a unique and immersive musical experience for attendees. The festival takes place at various venues in Salzburg, including the iconic Grosses Festspielhaus.

Rupertikirtag:

Rupertikirtag is a traditional folk festival held annually in honor of Saint Rupert, the patron saint of Salzburg. Taking place in late September, this lively event features a wide range of activities including live music performances, traditional dances, amusement rides, food stalls offering local delicacies, and a colorful parade through the streets of Salzburg. Travelers can immerse themselves in the vibrant atmosphere, interact with locals dressed in traditional costumes, and savor authentic Austrian cuisine.

Jazz & the City:

Jazz & The City is an annual music festival that transforms Salzburg into a vibrant hub for jazz enthusiasts. Held in October, this event showcases a diverse lineup of jazz musicians from around the world performing at various venues throughout the city. From intimate club settings to grand concert halls, travelers can enjoy a wide range of jazz styles and performances. The festival also includes workshops, jam sessions, and exhibitions, providing opportunities for both seasoned jazz lovers and newcomers to explore the genre.

Salzburg Whitsun Festival:

The Salzburg Whitsun Festival is a relatively new addition to the city's festival calendar, established in 1973 by conductor Herbert von Karajan. Taking place during the Pentecost weekend, this festival focuses on presenting opera productions and concerts with a specific theme each year. Renowned artists and ensembles collaborate to create exceptional performances that captivate audiences with their artistic interpretations. The festival takes place at various venues in Salzburg, including the Salzburg Festival Hall and the Haus für Mozart.

Salzburg Cultural Days:

Salzburg Cultural Days is an annual event that celebrates the city's cultural diversity through a series of exhibitions, performances, workshops, and lectures. Held in November, this event aims to promote dialogue and understanding between different cultures by showcasing their artistic expressions. Travelers can explore art exhibitions, attend dance and theater performances, participate in workshops, and engage in thought-provoking discussions on various cultural topics.

In conclusion, Salzburg offers a wide array of festivals and events throughout the year that cater to different interests and preferences. From classical music enthusiasts to folk festival lovers, there is something for everyone in this culturally vibrant city. Attending these festivals and events not only allows travelers to experience the rich cultural heritage of Salzburg but also provides an opportunity to immerse themselves in the city's lively atmosphere.

CHAPTER 11

Conclusion

Salzburg is a captivating destination that offers a unique blend of history, culture, and natural beauty. As a traveler, visiting this enchanting city will undoubtedly leave you with unforgettable memories and a deep appreciation for its rich heritage.

Salzburg's picturesque setting, nestled amidst the stunning Austrian Alps, provides a breathtaking backdrop for exploration. The city's well-preserved historic center, listed as a UNESCO World Heritage site, is a treasure trove of architectural wonders. From the iconic Hohensalzburg Fortress perched atop the Festungsberg hill to the charming Getreidegasse with its narrow lanes and ornate shop signs, every corner of Salzburg exudes charm and elegance.

For music enthusiasts, Salzburg holds a special allure as the birthplace of the legendary composer Wolfgang Amadeus Mozart. The city pays homage to its prodigious son through various attractions such as Mozart's Birthplace and Mozart's Residence, where you can delve into his life and musical genius. Additionally, Salzburg is renowned for its annual Salzburg Festival, a world-class celebration of music and performing arts that attracts artists and spectators from around the globe.

Beyond its cultural heritage, Salzburg also offers an abundance of natural beauty. The nearby Salzkammergut region boasts crystal-clear lakes, rolling hills, and idyllic landscapes that have inspired countless artists and writers throughout history. A visit to Lake Wolfgang or Lake Hallstatt is a must for those seeking tranquility and serenity amidst nature's splendor.

Furthermore, Salzburg's culinary scene is sure to tantalize your taste buds. From traditional Austrian delicacies such as Wiener Schnitzel and Sachertorte to international gourmet cuisine, the city offers a diverse range of dining options to suit every palate. Don't forget to pair your meal with a glass of locally produced wine or beer for an authentic culinary experience.

As you wander through Salzburg's streets, you'll also encounter a vibrant arts and crafts scene. From boutique shops selling handmade goods to bustling markets offering local produce and souvenirs, there are plenty of opportunities to immerse yourself in the city's creative spirit.

In summary, Salzburg is a destination that effortlessly combines history, culture, natural beauty, and culinary delights. Whether you're strolling through its charming streets, exploring its historic landmarks, or simply taking in the breathtaking scenery, this city will captivate your senses and leave you yearning for more.

I hope as a travel writer who has embedded my Salzburg knowledge and experience in this guide, I have been able to equip you with all the information you will be needing to embark on this journey? So pack your bags and embark on a journey to Salzburg – a place where history comes alive and dreams are realized.

Safe Trip!

Printed in Great Britain
by Amazon